This Much I Know...

The Space Between

Sue Bowles

This Much I Know...The Space Between by

Copyright - © - 2019 Sue Bowles

All rights reserved. No portion of this book may be reproduced in any form without permission from the publisher, except as permitted by U.S. copyright law. For permissions contact:

Scripture quotations taken from The Holy Bible, New International Version® NIV® Copyright © 1973 1978 1984 2011 by Biblica, Inc. TM Used by permission. All rights reserved worldwide

Cover by Eneas Nunez

Edited by Ali Cicerchi

Iron art by Mike Cox (mike.cox58@gmail.com)

Published by Sue Bowles PO Box 310 Pataskala, OH

www.mystepahead.com

Mystepahead1@gmail.com

Dedication

There is no getting around it. Life is just hard. And the essence of life is finding a way…making a way…choosing the way to have joy during the struggle. No one exemplifies that for me like Jimmy and Bethany Caudill.

Bethany lived with neuroendocrine cancer for 17 years. I met her the last two years of her life. Amid a ravaging disease, Bethany was full of joy and made me feel celebrated, important, and valued, right in the middle of the things this book discusses. She was a lighthouse to me. Bethany celebrated my little victories as if I had just climbed Mount Everest. She wept when I hurt, hugged when I was down, and just smiled. OH that smile!

As the disease began to take over, Bethany never lost her joy. She still sang with the worship team, using a cane or a chair for support if needed, but nothing was taking away her joy. Up to the last two weeks of her life she was continually asking "What's next?" in her treatment and setting goals…like singing with the worship team again. She had her days, but her focus was always right where it needed to be. As her life came to a close, she told Jimmy, her husband, that he needed to learn to lean INTO Christ in the midst of the pain, for that is where true joy lies. She lived that.

Bethany knew I was writing this book and encouraged me every step of the way. She did not live to see it become reality, but I feel her cheering me, gleaming at me, and oh…that smile! Jimmy and their son, Waylon, continue that joy. Jimmy has become a dear friend who is taking the sorrow of losing his wife and using it to get a degree to help other men navigate the choppy waters of being the caregiver to a spouse. Bethany's legacy lives on. These two sayings hung over her bed as she was escorted to the arms of Jesus, and Jimmy blessed me with them. It is my prayer this book is just one way to show what it means to "live like it's heaven on earth, love like you'll never be hurt."

Thank you, Jimmy and Bethany, for showing me how to navigate the space between. You model it well. It is to you this book is dedicated with all my love.

Contents

Acknowledgements
This Much I Know… Introduction 1
Chapter 1 Hurt People Hurting Their Kids 3
Chapter 2 Permanently Scarred 8
Chapter 3 Blazing New Trails 14
Chapter 4 Love Came Looking for Me 25
Chapter 5 The Adventure Begins 31
Chapter 6 Coming Out of the Dark 38
Chapter 7 Escape to the Woods 42
Chapter 8 A Good Thing Gone Bad 48
Chapter 9 Amanda 54
Chapter 10 Love Found Me! 60
The Space Between Introduction 68
Chapter 11 Own Your Story 70
Chapter 12 Grieve Your Story 78
Chapter 13 You ARE Valuable to God! 82
Chapter 14 You are HIS! 85
FINAL THOUGHTS 88
References 90
About the Author 91

Acknowledgements

When I set out to write this book in 2015, I had no idea what was going to come out…how long it was going to take…or WHAT it was going to take to be able to share my story. No one makes it through life alone, and my journey is no different. I am not the person I am today without the love and support of many people.

My parents, Tom and Dolores – I am SO proud to be your daughter. You set the bar for surviving and thriving. Through your challenges I have learned to overcome, because I have watched you do it. I am FOREVER grateful God chose you from among the crowd to give me life. I am the blessed one. I love you both SO much and I am so proud of you!

My siblings, Beth, Steve, Chris, and Scott – there are no words to express how much I treasure your support of, and belief in, me. You believed in me when this was just a dream. You watched me struggle and fight…and you helped me win. And you never once said I shouldn't share my story, which in some ways, is also part yours. We've done life together, and now we're all LIVING! There's no better feeling, and no better people, with whom I want to live! We are one strong bunch and we don't quit.

Ed Hyland and Amy Ginther – two Student Affairs professionals who said with their actions and their words that I mattered and had something to offer. I literally owe my life to you. Thanks for sharing my secret and setting me on the path to healing.

Billy Sprague – Thank you for ski lodge talks and ski slope walks, for recommended reading lists and teaching me to watch my steps. It's a long journey, Billy…and I'm going to make it!

Amanda Washel (Grace Recovery Counseling) – There is no other counseling office on the planet I would ever want to sit in! You had SO many 'firsts' with me, and I am beyond grateful. Thank you for your guidance, accountability, support, challenge, and asking the hard questions. God used you just as much as He used the Retreats.

He used you to bring me back to life. How do I ever say thank you for that?!

My Walking Stick Retreats family – you have walked this journey with me just like my biological family. You have shown me what love looks like – dirty, roll up your sleeves kind of love. You have been Jesus with skin on. Words escape me to adequately capture how God has used you. Thank you for accepting me and loving me, especially that first year. What an absolute joy and privilege it has been to go on the 'dam walk' with you and come out the other side!

The Leadership Team of Walking Stick Retreats – David Mullins, Kathy Sprinkle, Sam Howard, Elizabeth Lutz, Damon Seacott, and Steve Brummer – God has used you to show me His real thoughts of me. Thank you for setting the atmosphere where 'it's okay to not be okay' and to be authentic, mess and all. The retreats helped me find healing I never thought I'd have. God has used you mightily. This book is a snapshot of His work in me through you.

None of this would be possible without my relationship with Christ. It is THE most important thing in my life and makes this entire story make sense. If you're somewhere in 'the space between' and want to know more about Jesus Christ, contact me. It would be my honor to share more. I can be reached through my website, mystepahead.com.

This Much I Know...

Introduction

We all have a story. Your life is your story. Some of it may feel like a drama, other parts an adventure, other parts a thriller, and other parts a suspense.

Telling that story can be a challenge when life has thrown a lot of dirt your way. We lose ourselves in our story because all we see is the mess around us. We can't see ahead or around, and we certainly don't feel we have anything to offer. We lose hope and we lose our sense of purpose. Life becomes something to be endured, not something to be enjoyed.

No one can take from you your story. It is YOUR story, one worthy of being told, one NEEDING to be told. It is ongoing and always has another chapter to be written.

I struggled with my story for DECADES. I didn't like my story and I CERTAINLY didn't understand how anyone could benefit from hearing everything that had happened to me. All I saw was life passing me by with little to no hope of being able to find meaning in it beyond the pain. What I didn't realize is that each interaction, each relationship, each challenge, and each encouragement was building for me a foundation of hope, of belief, of 'just maybe…' Maybe I DID have worth. Maybe I DID have something to offer. Maybe I WAS more than what had happened to me. Maybe, just maybe, there WAS hope to find meaning and purpose, and dare I say it…joy!

I hope this book is one more encouragement along your journey. I want it to be for you what others were for me…a lighthouse in the middle of the storm, shining a little hope, a little light to get your bearings, to regroup and move on. I don't know a lot, but my story, what I have learned in life…***this much I know**…* and I am grateful to share it with you.

Chapter 1

Hurt People Hurting Their Kids

"They were hurt people hurting their kids." I've loved that phrase ever since I first heard it at a retreat in 2014. It made sense. It hit home. It validated my experiences, helping them make sense. It didn't condone anything; it just explained things from a proper perspective.

Mom and Dad did the best they could. I know this. But that still doesn't make it right. When your background is one of dysfunction - in whatever form it takes - it's unreasonable to think that anything BUT dysfunction would be passed on to your kids.

Dad grew up in an orphanage since age 12 when, because of the Great Depression, his parents had difficulty providing. Mom was the baby of six kids, all who struggled with image issues growing up…going to the "academy" and having to be a perfect "academy girl" took its toll. It all left its mark - on Mom and Dad…AND their kids.

Probably one of the greatest hurts in Mom and Dad's lives came in 1962 when they buried their firstborn son. Rusty had a birth defect around his liver and bile duct. I hear he was an absolute pistol and taught them much about how to live. Rusty died on December 22, 1962. Two days later, on Christmas Eve, Mom and Dad learned that Rusty's eyes had given two boys sight. OH how I wish I could meet those men and see the eyes of my brother.

Because of that great pain, Mom and Dad were in deep grief. Growing up, Christmas was a time of dread, at least for a few days. Dad would always be tense in the week leading up to Christmas, as was Mom. We just knew to expect it each year. It wasn't until I was little older, I came to understand the bigger picture. I also remember, however, the year when Mom and Dad came home from a marriage seminar and Dad said, "I finally let go of Rusty." Since then Christmases got better. Understanding their grief helps explain everything else.

Dysfunction is a crazy thing. When you're a child amid dysfunction, you don't know what's right or wrong...it just IS. Your reality. Your normal. Your secret. Your life. You learn the silent rules of don't talk, don't trust, and don't feel. Even as a young child you learn how to observe things and adjust. Something may have happened to cause a sibling to get yelled at. "Note to self: don't do _____." I remember as a teenager seeing a sibling get into a heated argument with Mom and Dad over something. I LITERALLY told myself "it will never happen to me," and I learned how to shut down emotionally. The problem with that, however, is that it kills you on the inside, and you don't even realize it until you're anesthetized and find yourself just trying to make it through the day, without drawing attention to yourself. Yet deeper down, you yearn for attention, validation, support, care, and ultimately, love.

My younger years were good. We had dinner at the table, my siblings and I were involved in sports, and we just had fun around the house. I love the memories of watching my brother Steve play soccer on Saturdays. When it was halftime, Dad would jog out onto the field with a bunch of kids and play goalie while we took shots on goal at him. Dad was involved and played with his kids. When it got colder, he would make his famous hot chocolate with milk and REAL cocoa - bakers cocoa. He would make a roux of the cocoa and water so it had the consistency of syrup, and he would heat up milk on the stove...slowly...stirring frequently...to avoid scalding. And then he would put the syrup in the bottom of our mugs and fill it with hot milk, stirring it until the proper mix was achieved. It was SO worth the wait. Every time.

Then there was the fudge. Every year we would make a day trip out of visiting the farm of a friend of Mom and Dad. We would ride the mini ponies and run around the fields and fulfill the main purpose: collect a BUNCH of black walnuts, still in the hulls. It was a mission we took seriously. We knew the reward: Dad's black walnut fudge! Dad would take over the kitchen and make this tremendous fudge with the fresh black walnuts. It took a lot of work to get the nuts out. If you've ever collected black walnuts when they fall from the tree, you know what I mean.

The fruit of the nut is inside a hard shell, and that hard shell is inside a hull which hangs from the tree branches. Once matured, the hulls fall to the ground. The hulls need to be spliced to let them dry out. Once dried out a bit, they are cut open and the hard shell removed. It will still have black on the outside of it. It's best to first use gloves, and second, let that dry out a bit. Then pull out a 16-ounce hammer and start cracking. Now, if a single recipe for fudge calls for a cup of walnuts, for example, you better get cracking...literally! It was truly a labor of love. He would stand in the kitchen and keep a watchful eye on the candy thermometer, faithfully stirring the "good stuff" until it was the right temp to pour into the pan. The hard part was waiting for it to cool so we could eat it. But we knew that was only temporary and the reward was well worth the wait. Black walnuts always make me smile. A few years ago, some friends from church had a bunch in their yard so I picked up a few trash bags full and worked the process. It was so much fun to give them to Dad and see his smile. Ahh...memories.

As I've grown older, I see things so much more clearly. I see how unacceptable certain things were growing up. I see how Dad's alcoholism and professional pressure took a toll on him. Things I was embarrassed about as they happened are now evidence of how bad it was. And the sad thing is...I didn't realize it at that time. The "rules" took over. The rationalizations for things were not reasonable.

I remember one period where there were roaches in the house. Mind you we kept the house clean - there was no junk or trash build up. We had clutter from seven folks under one roof (who wouldn't!), but there was a field nearby and bugs and mice liked to find their way in. Dad was a chemist and he had some powerful bugspray. But instead of calling in an exterminator to deal with the issue he would keep spraying his spray along the kitchen baseboards each night. It smelled a bit. I remember as a young teen being concerned about going into the kitchen for fear of seeing a scurrying bug - even one. I would stand on the carpet at the entryway, turn on the light, try not to look at the floor (though curiosity almost always won), and wait about five seconds before stepping into the kitchen. Logic would say call an exterminator. The rules said, "don't tell anyone - what would they think?" I even have that thought right now as I type! The rules don't die easily.

But I also see all that from a clear-headed review mirror angle. Dad was under a lot of pressure at work. He was VP and there was the pressure of performance and image. He felt he had to live up to it...live a way of life that was totally opposite of how he was raised and how he raised his family. Alcohol became the salve to the hurt inside - fear of failure and whatever else was going on - and when alcohol usage turns into alcoholism, all rationale goes out the window. I was just there when it happened.

I was involved in sports in junior high and high school. One summer, I played softball in an area league and was selected to the All-Star Team. I was a starter. We played in a few tournaments and one of them was in a neighboring town. We had been advancing and were in the "top 4." The family was coming to watch me play but ran behind, got there late, and got there only in time for the trophy presentation for third place. I played basketball my senior year of high school. It was my first time playing organized ball, so I wasn't very good. I didn't start but got some obligatory playing time each game. But the one thing I COULD do...I could cheer! I was going to be the biggest cheerleader that team had. I was always up on the bench yelling and clapping and waving my arms and cheering on my teammates. My shoelaces and shoes were even the school colors! I would go home hoarse each night after a game. And when you're in the school chorus that's not a good thing!

It was one of our last games of the season. No one from the family had been to any of my games to watch me play. The school was in downtown Dayton, eight miles from home and Mom and Dad both worked. It was the last home game of the year and all the seniors were starting. which meant I got to start! The family was coming, as was a favorite teacher. My boyfriend was in the stands. I had people coming to watch me, when no one had been there all year. I was feeling excited and special.

Warmups were done. The National Anthem was played. I kept sneaking glances at the stands. Still no one had showed up except the boyfriend. Team lineups were announced. I had my one shining moment to run from the bench, through the tunnel of high fives, to the center of the court. And no one except the boyfriend saw it. I played a few minutes into the game and then was taken out. My favorite teacher, Fr. Denny got there in a bit and asked Garry (boyfriend) if I had played yet. Garry told him I had already been taken out. I saw my family come through the gym doors and sit down. I was already on the bench. I didn't get put back in the entire game. What was cool, though, was that at our end of the season banquet, the award for "Most Spirited" was voted on by the team. They voted ME Most Spirited. Mom, Dad, and Fr. Denny were at the banquet when I found out and received my trophy...in front of a room full of family and teammates. That trophy still sits proudly on the shelf in my room. I may not have played, but I was an active participant. And it was appreciated.

Those are just a few things that come to mind when I think about growing up in a dysfunctional home. But somehow through all that heartache and pain, God was weaving together a tapestry and His plan for my life would not be halted or even delayed from humanness gone wild. Somehow, through ALL of this, He allowed me to be involved in the LIFE group at school (Living in Faith Experience) as well as the SEARCH retreat program through the Catholic Youth Organization. I was even on the leadership team for SEARCH. I had enough spiritual quest going on that He took the seeds planted and would continue to water them for the next couple years until they started to grow. I think these experiences give me better empathy toward others in abusive situations. I was almost 50 years old before I had a counselor help me face the fact that I grew up in an abusive situation. It took a while and a lot of work for me to put that label to it. I used to blow it off as "just dysfunctional" or "different". Never abusive. Even one of my brothers commented to me once that "we grew up in a 'different' home." It's still difficult to this day to call it abusive. So many preconceived notions. There wasn't physical abuse. It was mental and emotional. That is still so very difficult to say, and even more difficult to write! I am thankful I can see things through an adult's set of eyes now and realize "they were just hurt people hurting their kids."

I don't know how He does it, but ***this much I know*...** God is always at work and will turn our heartache into His heart for others.

Chapter 2

Permanently Scarred

A BOY NAMED BOBBY

There is much of my childhood I don't remember, but there is one day that is emblazoned in my mind. Try as I may for 16 years, I could not avoid the devastating truth. I am a childhood rape survivor. Before I share anything else, if you fear this could be triggering for you, you know enough to be able to skip right over this and still understand the rest of the book. Because if this is triggering for you, my sense is there has been personal experience with this subject as well. By all means take a break, engage in some self-care, and when you come back to the book, decide where you need to pick up. This section is written not only for me, but also for those who don't have personal experience or contact with a rape survivor. My hope is that you will be more aware of what survivors are going through and discover new ways of being supportive and helpful. I want my story to give courage to someone else.

I was in first grade. I was walking home from school one sunny afternoon. I don't remember what brought it on but Bobby Nolan, a blond-haired classmate, approached me.

"Come here. I want to show you something," he said. I was seven. Curiosity is normal, so I followed. There was absolutely no indication of anything about to happen.

Bobby led me to the woods, which were just past the sidewalk I was already walking on as I headed home after a day in first grade. What would happen over the course of the next 30-45 minutes forever changed my life.

Before I knew it, Bobby raped me. And not just once; twice. I was held against my will with my hands pinned down, told not to say anything to anyone, and told to be quiet when people were walking nearby. It was only when my mom came looking for me that I had my opportunity to escape. I was 45 minutes late coming home from school. She was scared. She loved me, and she came looking.

Bobby was still having his way when I heard her panicked voice from a distance, calling my name, hoping for a response. We only lived three-quarters of a mile from the school. It was the early 1970's and walking to school was normal. There was no reason to fear. Back then, it was safe and normal to walk to school.

"That's my Mom calling. I have to go!" I told Bobby. By now, the schoolyard was empty and there were no voices anywhere to be heard so my Mom's voice echoed throughout the trees. Mom's voice was my reason to escape. At that moment, I was stronger than Bobby because I had my opportunity - my excuse - to escape. He had held me against my will long enough. I scrambled to my feet, got dressed and Bobby's last words were "don't tell anybody." He went the other direction and left me to fend for myself. He used me, cast me aside, and went on with his life, while mine became frozen in time.

I can only imagine the thoughts that pulsed through Mom's mind. All she knew was her 7-year-old daughter was late coming home from school and there was no reason known for that to happen. I walked out of the woods - alone - not knowing what had happened, what I was feeling, or what was going to happen next. As any 7-year-old would, I became scared I'd be in trouble for not going straight home from school. And again, I didn't know what had just happened. I had no words. I had no knowledge of anything, no context to put it in. This wasn't something that was talked about in that day, and it wasn't even thought of as a possibility...ESPECIALLY with an elementary-aged boy!

My mom reacted to my being late, like any other scared parent would, and because I had no words for what happened, I had no way of telling her something terrible had just taken place. As it turned out, that day wouldn't come until decades later. I remember going home and I was grounded for the rest of the day. She told Dad that I was late coming home and she had to go find me, but I don't remember much of his reaction. After that, my emotions became frozen in time. My head and heart always knew something had happened but isn't it sad how the mind buries things to survive? I don't know what it was that finally drew it out of me in 1986, but I'm glad it did.

MORE BROKENNESS, MORE SCARS

For years, I felt angry toward my mom. I felt she was trying to break into my life when I wanted my independence. I remember being on a SEARCH retreat and the last day of the event feeling as if a rock was being thrown through the window when I had to leave and go home. Mom was always trying to pull out what I was feeling about whatever. She was seemingly always making a statement like "don't hide your feelings." Well, hiding my feelings was how I survived because I didn't know what the landslide of emotions inside me was - or how to handle them - so I didn't want to let on to anyone how I was feeling. I didn't want to deal with the questions, and more so, I didn't want to have to think about what the possible answers could be. I. JUST. WANTED. TO. BE. LEFT. ALONE. Period.

Now, I'm confident some of that was just part of being a teenager, but part of it was from a subconscious belief that no one cared and that I didn't matter. As our family grew and we kids started to have busier schedules and activities, Mom went back to work. It was commonplace to come home to an empty house. We kids had our routine...get a snack, watch some TV, and when we had pushed the envelope far enough, wipe down the back of the television with a cold cloth (so Dad couldn't tell we were watching TV rather than doing housework) and quickly get our housework done before he got home from work. But what I didn't realize at the moment is what we lived under: fear. We didn't want to get in trouble or get yelled at. I didn't realize the effect everything was having on me until Junior year of high school.

My Great Aunt Adele (Mom's aunt) lived in a nursing home and we would drive two hours to visit her. I still remember the odor of the floor...walking past certain rooms there was a strong smell of urine. Seeing folks sitting - or slumping - in their wheelchairs, alone, broke my heart. As I was already stuffing my emotions, I really didn't know how to handle seniors in a nursing facility. During one visit we were on the floor enjoying seeing Aunt Adele, and I walked down the hall past a room. A resident had slipped down in her wheelchair and was calling repeatedly for someone to help her. "Help! Help me!" was heard four or five times, and yet no one responded. That moment tipped the delicate scale of balance in my head - to the negative. I clearly remember thinking "No one cares. If no one cares, I don't want to live." Before I knew it was having suicidal thoughts.

I don't remember how long it went on. I distinctly remember emotionally "flipping the switch" before I would walk in my house. I was depressed and becoming more suicidal, convinced I didn't matter and no one cared. Yet, I would stop on the porch outside the house before I opened the front door coming home from school, take a deep breath, literally fake a smile, and walk through the door as if I was okay. Little did anyone know I was already dying on the inside.

Then one day at school, I must have said something to a friend. I don't remember what it was - probably something along the lines of "no one cares and maybe I'd be better off dead." You know, just your ordinary teenage comment! My friend, unbeknownst to me, had told a teacher - Mr. Kayne - and as soon as the last bell rang, he came running down the hall to find me. He brought me into the department's office and talked with me. I don't remember what I said, but he obviously had heard I was thinking of killing myself. We talked for a while and then he let me go. What I didn't know is that someone was calling my parents.

A day or two had gone by when I got a message at the school not to take the bus because Mom was coming to school to pick me up. That rarely happened so I knew something was up, yet I knew there was no escaping. "Resistance is futile," as they say. I had a job and had to be at work after school so when Mom came to get me, I was guarded and suspicious. I imagine we did a lot of small talk on the way home but as we got closer, Mom said she had something she wanted to talk with me about, so we went to Sinclair Park, a small park less than a mile from where I worked. We pulled off to the side somewhere, and I just stared out the window. Then she said, "Someone told me you were thinking of killing yourself. What's wrong? What's going on?" My secret was out, and I wasn't getting out of this one.

How do I tell my mom that visiting her aunt at the nursing home and hearing the resident repeatedly call for help, with no response from anyone, makes me think no one cares?! I didn't want her to be afraid of taking me to see Aunt Adele again. All of this was going through my head.

Knowing I didn't want to say anything about what I thought was the "real" cause, I told Mom, "We're all just so busy at the house. It's like we have a revolving front door." Wow! That was bold! At the time, I was thinking I was giving Mom a smokescreen, but now I have come to see I was really telling her the truth. I felt my family was too busy, that we didn't interact or have time for each other, that we didn't communicate, and that I didn't matter as a result. I was really telling her the dark truth of my pain.

Mom's reaction, however, shut me down quickly. When I unknowingly shared the true reason for my pain and loneliness and desire for attention, Mom got defensive. I clearly remember her saying "Well, you understand why it has to be that way don't you?" There was NO acknowledgement of what I was saying or trying to communicate. No comment on the deep pain and loneliness I had just let seep past all my defenses. If anything, my comment about people not caring was only supported. And that made it worse.

I faked it and told her I understood. I said I was okay and that talking helped. I lied through my teeth! I just wanted it to be over so I could go to work and forget any of this ever happened. I didn't believe people cared so the whole conversation seemed a farce to me. I don't know what she told Dad. I don't recall Dad saying anything specific about it except maybe when I went to bed. He expressed his love for me and that he was glad Mom and I had talked. Dad grew up in an orphanage during his teen years and has never been one to express a lot of emotion, so while it may seem little to most, to me, what he said was huge. It was Dad code for I love you and I care about you.

It's vitally important to say right now that my parents did the best they could. Remember that line from the start of this - "they were hurt people hurting their kids." None of this was intentional. It was all they knew to do. They did not have the tools to communicate in ways we have now. Our relationship wasn't as solid as it is now. I was too hurt and scarred to be able to do anything about how we communicated. Remember when I said my emotions were frozen in time? I was so far detached from my emotions that I couldn't tell you what I was feeling. I would just act it out, silently hoping someone would notice, someone would care. Because that would silence all the voices in my head telling me the opposite.

Perspective changes with distance. I tried a geographic cure by going to college almost three hours from home. While there, I tried to bury my pain in busyness and activities...anything to be seen. No matter what I did, my wounds followed me. Scars are healed wounds. We can't have scars without wounds. But when wounds are still bleeding it leaves you drained...physically and emotionally. And that pain needs to find a way out. Mine came out in drinking, swearing, an eating disorder, depression, anger, isolation. At one point when I was depressed after the death of a friend, I even started to cut myself. However, in true "denial" form, I wasn't cutting...I was "making marks on my arm." Some things die slowly, and denial is one of those things for me.

In so many ways, I was trapped in my wounds. I was permanently scarred by the crap life had thrown at me. Any ONE of those things is a lot for anyone to handle, but for some reason, in my life I've experienced all of them...and still more. There was ongoing sexual abuse by a neighborhood boy when I was in junior high and early high school, and I never told anyone. There were a lot of guys in high school who took advantage of me in some ways while on dates. This all laid the foundation in my life to believe I was unlovable, unworthy, had nothing of value to offer anyone, would always be on the outside looking in, and would always wonder if I'd ever be "good enough" for anything. I did not think highly - or healthily - of myself, and it showed in my actions toward myself. Little did I know that years later God would totally turn all those lies on their heads!

This much I know...no matter what happens, God sees, God knows, and God is at work to make good come out of even unspeakable horrors.

Chapter 3

Blazing New Trails

I like to think of myself as a trailblazer. I've chartered a lot of courses in my family...some I don't want to repeat, while others have led me places I never thought possible. One such path was college.

There are six kids in our family. In order of age, my siblings are Beth, Rusty (deceased at age 2), Steve, then me, Chris, and Scott. After high school, Beth went to college for a bit wanting to be a nurse. She did not finish and entered the workforce and eventually got an apartment with a friend. Steve was the first in our family to go away to school. He went to Ball State University in Indiana to study journalism. I was next. I graduated high school 2 two years after him and went to Defiance College. Neither Chris nor Scott have attended college.

I was a late bloomer. It was probably around Christmas of my senior year of high school or so before I finally started getting serious about looking at colleges. That's not to say they weren't already looking for me! My mail was packed every day with another letter or catalogue from a college. My ACT composite score was 26...a decent composite score in the early 80s. I was just too busy playing basketball and working to start thinking about my future. My thoughts at that point were simply "who will see me in my uniform today during school so I feel like I belong...at least in this moment?"

I knew I didn't want to go to a big college. I don't do well being a number and not a name. I was a messed-up student and silently needed to know I would be "seen", thereby validating my existence. I didn't think I could get that on a big campus. The college I was REALLY interested in was Adrian College in MI. But just looking at the out- of- state tuition made it cost prohibitive. You see...Mom and Dad didn't have a lot of extra money sitting around to pay for our schooling.

So then, I eventually received something in the mail from a little college in NW Ohio. It seemed nice. I liked the pictures. I don't recall what it was that started the ball rolling but one thing led to another and in the spring, I visited the campus. I still remember that trip with Mom and Dad. It was a Saturday and it was sunny...warm. We made the three-hour trek up the interstate, wound through the small country roads and little towns and were quickly reassured that we were in farm country! When we finally arrived, I was a mixture of excitement and disappointment. The main campus was only about two blocks long it seemed. I remember driving around the block to find a parking spot, seeing the campus pass by the window, and thinking "That's it? That's all the bigger it is?!"

We did the whole deal...met with Admissions, went on a tour, met a professor, ate lunch in the cafeteria. At that point, I wanted to go into Accounting. Why? Because I took it senior year of high school and liked it. I mean...isn't that how everyone else decides the course for your life?! C'mon...it was fun! However, that didn't last long.

I must have liked what I saw and heard. I don't think it was long after my visit that I applied. At that time, there were no college essays or anything that had to be written. It was basic stuff. One day I came home and there was an envelope on the kitchen table for me from Defiance College. It seemed rather thick, but I didn't know what to expect. I tore it open and started to cry. Mom and Dad were there. I just looked at them and said, "I got accepted. I'm going to college!"

I didn't really have a good read on what I wanted to do with my life. I just knew I wanted - needed - to get out of the house. Something wasn't right, and I thought a geographical cure would fix it.

Move-in day freshman year ended up being the same day Steve had to be back at school in Indiana. We loaded up our car (I think it was the Grenada at the time) with his stuff and some of my stuff. Mom and Dad were in front, Steve and I were in the back, with our first load of stuff crammed in the trunk. and I think maybe a car top carrier. We drove the couple of hours to Ball State and helped him return for his sophomore year. We didn't know at that point it would be his last. When we were done in Muncie, we again took to the highway up to the northern half of Indiana, cut across at Fort Wayne, and headed toward Defiance. Amazingly, I got there within the "arrival" window. We got checked in, went to the dorm, and moved in before starting two days of orientation.

It was a crazy time. I had no idea what I was doing. I latched on to whatever group of students I could find. I just needed security. And a friend.

I made it through orientation and registration. Classes began. I had my advisor for my Accounting I professor. It wasn't long before my issues started coming to the top. And not just in her class. I was a messed-up college kid, confused, hurting, lonely, and not knowing how to ask for help. So, I did what anyone else in that situation would do: I acted out.

SOMETHING ABOUT ED

It was only a few weeks into the semester...maybe a month...when I was walking across campus and Darby saw me. Darby was a Sig Ep (Sigma Phi Epsilon, the fraternity I was to become a little sis of) and worked as a night desk attendant in the Student Union, where the Dean of Students office was located. He called to me from across the Quad and asked if I had talked to Lucy, the Dean's secretary. I had said no, and he gave me the gut-wrenching news that the Dean of Students was looking for me. Let's see...small campus, 1000 students, only one cafeteria and that being down the hall from the Dean's office. Yep. I was screwed. No running now.

Being the dutiful student I was (following the pattern of being a dutiful daughter), I walked over to the Union and went into Lucy's office. She said the Dean had been trying to contact me and asked if I could wait until he came back from the Admin building just across the way. About 5 minutes later the Dean walked through the door and said in an upbeat way, "There is she is! She was hired to find her and there she is. C'mon in Sue." I wasn't quite sure what to expect. The Dean knew my name and face and I didn't even know who the man was. All that was about to change. I was about to find the person who would be a major influence in my life.

There was something about Ed that just really made me feel like he cared...and not because it was his job. He ended up being someone with whom I spent a lot of time talking. While the initial conversation had to do with my attendance in a class (my major -- you know, the one my Advisor taught!), and trying out for the basketball team, our future conversations got to be deeper...at my initiation. I would make an appointment to see him and he basically became a counselor for me. We would talk a couple hours at a time. He would sit in the chair next to mine with an end table between, prop his feet up on his desk, pull out a cigarette and blow smoke rings. And he would challenge me. He could quickly tell I was a confused college kid, but I was willing to let him pour into me and he was willing to help and listen. Ed taught me life skills. I remember when we talked about keeping a planner and time management. He asked what my objection was to having a planner, and I said, "I don't want to be a robot." He simply said, "Well I guess I'm a robot." It was those "little" things that are so huge to an 18- year- old away from home for the first time. And he just talked with no condemnation but with acceptance. Ed became my confidant, my counselor, my encourager, my listening ear. Over the years, he helped me through whatever was on my mind. What started out as the Dean talking with a student about the benefit of going to class turned into a four-year relationship which most likely got me through college.

SEARCHING FOR SIGNIFICANCE

There was so much junk going on in my life I'm amazed anyone wanted to talk with me. I quickly got a reputation for always being injured. I was the pitcher in the annual first day of class co-ed softball game in the Quad between the dorms and sprained my arm when I snagged a hard line drive. A different time, we were again playing softball and someone from the third floor thought my head had a bullseye on it and dumped water on it....and laughed....as did those around me. That same year, one day it was raining and I was running across campus, hit a split in the sidewalk and severely sprained my ankle. I was in a cast and on crutches. Try living on the third floor of the dorm on crutches and not having an elevator. Junior year I was taking Ceramics and liked being in the art room at midnight. I was on the kick wheel and injured the cartilage on the underside of my kneecap and had to walk in a knee immobilizer for two weeks to avoid surgery.

My insecurities were running my life by the time I got to college. They were just cloaked by "creative outlets." I was OVER involved in college. And I do mean O.V.E.R! I quickly became involved in several campus activities and by junior year was a leader in a number of them. But the emotional torrents underlying everything started to eke out. I started drinking...and by the time sophomore year came along my friends started making comments like "There are a lot of beer cans coming out of that room." I was searching for belonging, friends, and acceptance. I was a "little sis" of a fraternity and one night we had the annual Yucca Flatz party...grain alcohol and fruit punch. There is STILL a 10-minute span of my life I don't remember - the walk back from the party to the residence hall. Someone had asked to borrow a notebook and two days later, I was trying to remember where I put it. Thankfully that someone returned it.

You name it; I probably had a hand in it. I was working two campus jobs (total of 20 hours a week when 10 was considered full time), taking a full load - if not overload - of classes, little sis of a fraternity, joined a sorority Junior year, section editor of the school paper, college radio station DJ, and was on the Student Activities leadership board - just to name a few! One year I coordinated three major events - Homecoming, Winter Formal, and the 18-hour Muscular Dystrophy Dance-a-thon. I remember the dance-a-thon because I had about four hours of sleep in 60 hours, and I was doing Mt. Dew and No-Doz. I bumped into a couch in the student union lounge, fell onto it and fell asleep and when I awoke, I had THE WORST charley horse in my calf! I never claimed I was taking care of myself.

I was trying SO hard to find acceptance and approval through being seen. I was insecure, so to hide that I put on the facade of confidence. I was hurting and I put on the mask of happiness. By the time junior year rolled around it, pretty much caught up to me.

JUNIOR YEAR = STRESS!

My roommate was Reagan Dunlavy. We called her Ronnie for short. She was fun-loving and wouldn't let me get away with talking down to myself. A group of five of us had formed a little group the prior year - even had shirts made - and we called ourselves the Misfits. Thinking back to that it just screamed pain - from ALL of us. Even in that group, though, I was the fifth one - the cog in the wheel it seemed. The group's name screamed anger or hurt, and it started to come out.

Ronnie became my roomie the year following all this, and we seemed to hit it off. There was something about her challenging me.

I remember her explicitly saying, "Don't ever call yourself a misfit again!" She was serious! She was having none of it! I worked at the campus pizza shop so at the end of the night I could bring home any pizza I wanted. Ronnie and her friend Ange were waiting to place the order and we stayed up eating pizza and of course - drinking beer.

This was the year I coordinated Homecoming and Ronnie was chosen as the Freshman delegate. She was popular and well-liked, but there was one little problem: she had folks telling her she was an alcoholic. One night Ronnie went missing. I got concerned and a few friends and I went looking for her in the middle of the night. We walked the mile to downtown Defiance and couldn't find her. I honestly don't remember where she ended up, but she was in a drunken fog and had gone walking and returned hours later.

There was another incident where things got a little out of control. One night when I was sleeping, Ronnie and Ange decided to marker my face. When I woke up, I had black marker all over my face. They had given me bushy eyebrows, a beard and mustache...it was cruel. I was hurt and angry. I called my folks and that Sunday, they made the three hour trek to Defiance to check on me and talk to our Hall Director. I then talked to the Director later and she went to the Dean of Students about it - yes, Ed - the same Dean who was my confidant. I was given the opportunity to "cite" Ronnie - have her written up to send her through judicial. My response was simply "No. Citing Ronnie is like citing my sister. We'll work it out."

We finished the semester and after Christmas break, I came back and all of Ronnie's stuff was gone. There were a couple things left on my desk with a note. She had left school to go to Hazelden in Minnesota for alcoholism treatment. I was sad and scared. Ronnie was finally the first person I fit in with socially. A lot of my felt needs were met through her - acceptance, social life, laughter, challenge, companionship. I felt like I was back to freshman year trying to figure out where I fit in.

My new roomie wasn't quite the same. She came from a well-off family and we were just very different. It wasn't bad but we weren't the kind of friends that would hang out together. So, when the opportunity to pledge Beta Sigma came up Spring Semester - and they asked if I would live at the house because they had to have a certain number - I took it. I can't say that was the greatest decision I ever made - living at the sorority house as a pledge, with an active member as my roommate. Yeah. Issues. And one of those issues caused me to lose that friendship.

Pledging was six weeks of fun and camaraderie as well as hard work. There was a big flood in town so in the middle of the night we took care of our community service requirement by helping sandbag the one bridge in town to keep the road open to the hospital. I remember walking down streets going door-to-door in the dark and being told to be careful in case there were open manholes. Minor detail! We had a lot of fun - the typical fun you have during pledging. We pimped the house one night and RAN for our lives. It was epic! The next morning when we had our pledge march and time at the house, we had to clean it all up. While the actives acted like they were angry they would quietly tell us "great job – I've never seen a pimp THAT good!" Of course, we all got thousands of demerits - which meant absolutely nothing other than making the actives feel like they were doing their job.

For the last year and a half of my college career I lived at the Beta Sigma house. I have so many stories I could tell on myself but must keep those private, though they bring a smile to my face just remembering. I'm not saying I was a model student. I was still doing my homework from 10p-2a, getting up at six in the morning to be first to breakfast at 7:15, and then taking classes starting at 8a and working and then student activities..........and the cycle continued. While I FINALLY had the external look like I had found my identity - my sorority letters on my chest - I was still lonely and aching on the inside.

The year I pledged my psychology professor thought I might be slipping into clinical depression and sent me in for an evaluation. The psychologist didn't think I was depressed but just stressed out and needed a break. This was in March of my junior year, right before Spring break and right after pledging was done. I remember telling Ed, the Dean of Students, that I wasn't going to take a break. You see, if I went home due to being overstressed, it would cause too many questions and issues at home and I didn't know how to handle it. I would rather stick out the last six weeks of the semester and clear my head during the summer than must answer questions at home. They couldn't know what was going on. I didn't WANT them to know!

Due to financial concerns, each year I never knew if I would be able to return to Defiance. I wanted to...but it was a matter of how much financial aid I would receive on top of a student loan. So, like every year before, I stopped by Ed's office to say goodbye. As always, he was encouraging, and we talked about how things had gone for the year. He expressed concern that I get a break over the summer and hoped I would return in the fall for senior year refreshed and renewed.

TURNING POINT!

That summer, before senior year, was different for me. I didn't want to take a gym class at Defiance. Most folks took swimming and that just wasn't my thing. I was NOT keen on being seen in a bathing suit, it was a night class, and it just wasn't happening. To make up for it, I started taking gym classes at Sinclair Community College after sophomore year. Due to the transfer rate of credits, I had to take three classes to get the full number of credits needed to fulfill the graduation requirement for graduation.at Defiance. The year prior I had taken a self-defense class and really enjoyed it. The second year I took a tennis class and then a running class. I rode the bus to get downtown at six o'clock in the morning so I could get there early to practice tennis - especially my serve. The running class was fun as I enjoyed running anyway. Between classes, working, and guitar group at church, I had a full schedule. But the summer between junior and senior years of college was different as I had a significant life change which made that summer different: on May 31, 1985, I gave my life to Christ at a Petra concert in Dayton, Ohio.

It took a year for me to realize my lifestyle needed to change but I made external changes. I got a perm instead of the straight brown hair I had lived with up to that point. I got contacts. No more big-lensed glasses. I got new clothes. It was fun doing a "fashion show" for Dad on the back deck when Mom and I got home. And it was even more fun totally messing with people when I returned to school. People didn't recognize me! I remember walking into the lounge in the Student Union and someone asking if I was new, etc. As I left someone said, "Who was that?" and someone said "Sue Bowles! I didn't recognize her!" Maybe, just maybe, I found my new identity.

When I got back to school, I also realized very quickly that Ed was no longer in his office in the Union. I was told that he had taken a promotion and now was the VP for Advancement and had an office in the President's Office area. GULP! I wasn't sure I wanted to trek over there and let it be known to a new office of people that he was basically my counselor. I felt VERY awkward having to go through a different secretary who didn't know me or why I wanted to see him. Because when you think about it, what does a current student have to do with the VP of a college charged with fund-raising?! However, one day I bit the bullet and stopped by to see him and he welcomed me. We talked, and he shared about his promotion, etc., but said he would still be available to me. That meant a lot and was very helpful. I didn't see him as frequently as before. In the prior year I probably met with him about once a week or so, and Senior year it went down to a couple times a month. But when we talked, we talked at length...a couple hours at a time

By the time Spring semester rolled around, Ed's conversations with me started to take a different turn. He knew I wasn't ready to go out into the workforce. He knew I had few plans, so he started giving me homework projects. They were good ones that made me think and write out comparisons, so I could visually see the things going on in my head. He kept them all in a file. But there was one day that changed the course of my life. I still remember the main part of the conversation as if it were yesterday.

I don't remember specifically what his homework for me had been, but we were talking about it and he asked a question. I went off on some crazy monologue and at the end said, "well when society tells you to not say anything..." and my voice trailed off as I closely inspected the weave pattern in his office carpet. He was silent for a moment and then asked what would become the door that opened the avalanche.

"Sue, did your parents hurt you?"

"No. Not them."

"Someone else?" Ed sensitively asked.

I kept staring at the floor and, with as much courage as I could muster, quietly said, "yea." I still hadn't looked him in the eye.

He took a breath and asked the next hardest question: "What happened?"

He knew he had a student in his office who was about to let out a HUGE secret - so huge that she had never let on to it in three years. He was patient and focused and deeply concerned as I told him about being raped in first grade. He expressed his sympathies and made sure I was OK and as we talked, I remember him saying "I wish I had known this sooner. It answers a lot of questions." Oddly enough, I was not taken aback by that statement. I was just glad someone finally knew. I had kept it a secret for 15 years. Ed was the first person I had told.

I had continued periodically seeing a counselor at the local counseling agency over the years. Ed knew this and asked if I had told my counselor. When I told him no, he strongly suggested I tell him my counselor at my next appointment which was the following week. I don't remember a lot about how the conversation ended, but I do remember walking back across campus feeling like the whole world suddenly knew. It seemed to me, in my paranoid mind, that each person who passed me on the sidewalk was looking straight through me, and "I was raped!" was painted on my face. It was horrifying and traumatic! And it was only the beginning.

A few days passed and I contacted Ed. I asked if he would go with me to my next counseling appointment and be there with me when I told the story again. It didn't take long for him to agree. He drove me. I remember him walking from his office area with a manila folder in his arm. When he set it down in his car, I saw it contained all the projects he had me work on. GULP! It was past the point of no return now.

When we got to the counselor's office, I introduced Ed and they chit chatted for a minute. Then Evan, the counselor, asked how I was, and I said "fine." The soft shoe dance began. Evan tried but I wasn't really talking. He could tell something was up and knew I had brought Ed for a reason but didn't know why.

Evan turned to Ed and said, "What do you think?"

Ed quietly but directly looked at me and simply said, "I think Sue needs to quit shadow-boxing and tell you what she told me." That was it. No hiding now!

At that point, the ball was in my court. I honestly don't remember the rest of the conversation. I don't remember much about the ride home other than looking out the window fearing what others thought if they saw me getting out of Ed's car. I don't really remember much of my conversations with Ed the rest of the year. I remember getting a picture with him at graduation and crying because I was afraid I'd never see him again. He was special. He had broken through my wall. He wanted only the best for me, and he dug deep to help that come out. I didn't know that was only the start.

MORE ISSUES, MORE SEEDS

One thing I didn't realize is that while in college, in addition to developing the start of a drinking problem, I had also developed an eating disorder. DC had one cafeteria. Everyone from the campus ate there and there were limited windows for meals, so if you missed the window, you missed the meal. Because I felt so awkward socially and had few folks I could sit with during meals, I pretty much ended up eating alone most every meal, at least until I joined the sorority and then ran track senior year. For the first two and a half years I felt like I was on display. I would go through the line, get what I needed from the condiment / salad / drink areas, and try to find a seat in an obscure corner in the least populated side of the cafeteria.

What happened next is sad to me, in retrospect. As I got more uncomfortable in my own skin, the fact that I was eating alone began to get blown up in my mind. Before I knew it, I had convinced myself that everyone in the cafeteria was watching me when I got up, and even though I was hungry and may have enjoyed another serving, the anxiety was more than I could control. I instead learned to shut off my hunger. Instead of going up for more where everyone would see that I was hungry, I shut off the hunger, dumped my tray, and got the heck out of dodge. Sometimes very hurriedly. I learned to survive the "all eyes are on me" phenomenon by shutting off my hunger. While that helped me survive at the time, it was really turning into an eating disorder that wouldn't be diagnosed until YEARS later. I passed it off as odd eating behaviors, but I was lying to myself.

My college years were wrought with trauma and struggle - pain from the inside being shown on the outside. Yet through it all, looking back now, I see God's hand. I had issues...and LOTS of them...but each one became an avenue through which seeds were planted for Him to show His fierce love.

This much I know...God is always at work. Even when we don't see it.

Chapter 4

Love Came Looking for Me

My family attended Catholic church all throughout my childhood. I am forever grateful to my parents for the investment in my life, via the quality education I received. The only time I went to public school was kindergarten, first grade, and sixth grade, when we lived across the street from a public school. The next year desegregation and bussing were enacted, and Mom and Dad said, "We didn't move across the street from a school for you to be bussed 30 minutes to another school," so they enrolled me and my two younger brothers in the elementary school our church ran. I attended for my junior high years, which at that time was defined as seventh and eighth grades.

Part of being an adult member of a Roman Catholic church is agreeing your kids will receive ongoing religious education called CCD, or Confraternity of Christian Doctrine. If the children attended the Catholic school then the required religion classes during school met that requirement, If the children attended public school, or any other non-Catholic school, they were expected/required to attend CCD classes held sometime during a weekday evening. So, when I was in sixth grade, I had to attend CCD classes once a week. It was like my first-ever night class, long before I made it to college.

The best part of that year was meeting my best friend, Kris. She and I would go on to become great friends. We had sleepovers at each other's homes and had quite a few adventures (including, I confess, some late-night neighborhood pranks which I would NOT recommend these days!). I learned how to make chip dip from soup mix and sour cream when I was at Kris' house. I learned about vitamins because Mom Krzyminski would set out a daily vitamin regimen for her kids each morning. Kris and I had a lot of "after the lights are off" conversations. She called my parents "Mom" and "Dad," and I called her parents the same. She is a special friend, and it all started in CCD class.

I was always the "religious" one in the family. I remember riding the bus into the parking lot of the school in either 7th or 8th grade, and as we drove past the convent (where the nuns lived) I remember thinking to myself "I'm going to live there someday." I was involved in a group the school called the God Squad. We would do service projects at least once a month after school, including nursing home visitations where we would not only visit the residents but also do other volunteer work there.

The Catholic education continued through high school. The elementary school was a "feeder school" to the Catholic high school located in downtown Dayton, Ohio. Families received a tuition discount if you came from one of the Catholic schools in Dayton. The high school was about eight miles from our house, and we rode public transportation to get there. We walked a mile to the bus stop in the pre-dawn hours with a backpack full of books. But no, it wasn't uphill both ways...only on the way home. I was involved in chorus, marching band, basketball, and drama in my time at Chaminade-Julienne High School, or CJ for short, and made some fantastic memories. I was in South Pacific at the University of Dayton my freshman year, playing Ngana, the little Polynesian girl. To this day I remember the lyrics to the opening scene where me and my "brother" were on stage.

I was also a very confused high school kid starving for attention and one particular year got wrapped up with some questionable friends. I believed a lot of their lies and had I acted on those, I would have gotten in trouble. The underlying themes in my life of wanting to be "seen," to validate my existence, and to have some worth had taken root and were growing. I now see all of that was a byproduct of living in a dysfunctional home.

Private school education is expensive at any point, and when you have two kids in high school and two more in grade school it gets even MORE expensive, even with the multiple child discount! One expectation in our family was that when you were old enough you would get a job and pay half of your tuition. For me, at that time, half of tuition was $500. I realize some may be aghast at the thought of parents expecting their kids to pay for their education while still a teen. I am all for having some "skin in the game," and I don't regret or resent any part of it.

There was a new fast food restaurant opening and they were taking applications. I was working the church festival and had planned to put in some applications that Saturday afternoon. I walked in, completed the application and had an on-the-spot interview. It went well and by the time I left I had been hired and given my uniform. I was ecstatic all the way on the walk home. When I entered the house, Dad was there and I said "Well, it's going to be a long time before I apply anywhere again." He was concerned and asked what happened. I went up the steps, tried my best to hide my smile, and showed him my uniform as I said, "Because I got a job!" He was so happy for me! Thus began a few years where I would learn much about customer service, much about myself, and meet someone who would be used by God to literally change my life.

That someone would be Buddy Hurwood. Buddy was a cook, and I don't remember much about our getting to know each other but we were friendly toward each other. I honestly don't even remember if Buddy and I ever went out on a date before the one, life-changing night. But I do remember that night, and even more than 33 years later, I still celebrate it every year.

I had gone away to college after high school graduation, so I would come back to work at the same place mainly during the summers and sometimes over the holiday break at Christmas. It was during the summer of 1985 when one special evening became forever etched in my mind.

Buddy had asked me to go to a concert with him. He asked if I was familiar with a band named Petra, a Christian rock band. I was vaguely familiar only because one of the student groups I belonged to at college played some of their music. Buddy asked if I would like to go to the concert with him as they were coming to town, playing at a venue 10 minutes from where we worked. I agreed, not sure what I was getting myself into. Now mind you, I had only been to one or two concerts in my life up to this point in time, the summer before my senior year of college!

The place was packed out and we had decent seats - first section off the floor right next to the railing...in essence no one was in our way. I was a little reserved at the start, but it didn't take long before I was clapping and dancing like the rest of the crowd. There was something different about this group. There was an energy, a joy, an enthusiasm that seemed to go well beyond just a great concert. And all the songs were about Jesus Christ and being a Christian. It was cool, but it was kind of weird. People were raising their hands as they sang. We didn't do this in Catholic school or Mass!

As the concert ended the singer spoke for a bit. He started to share something I had never heard put the way he explained it. He talked about how Jesus died for my sins so I didn't have to pay the price for them, and that if I had never accepted Christ into my heart before I could do it right then.

"Accepted Christ." I had heard that phrase and even discussed it with folks at college. A year prior to all this there was a basketball handler named Tanya Crevier who had come to campus to do her show. She was staying in the dorm down the hallway from me, so I wrote her a letter. I told her I was "religious" but wasn't too sure about this "accepting Christ" thing. She wrote me back and shared a bit which really encouraged me. I still have that letter. Who knew what started that day would continue to grow into a friendship with Tanya? I can say that Tanya was my "first touch" in learning about Christ past my religion. My attitude had always been "show me in the Bible where it says I have to accept Christ to get to Heaven. That's not what my religion says!" I thought anyone who talked about "accepting Christ" was just a Bible thumper, and I wanted nothing to do with them. I had my own beliefs and wasn't ready for anything else to infiltrate them. Or so I thought.

They say music is the universal language, and I believe that to be true. There was something about the music at the concert which spoke to me in places and in ways I didn't expect. By the time the singer got done praying and invited anyone who had accepted Christ to a back room, I looked at Buddy and said, "Let's GO!" I didn't quite know what I was going back to do but again, like a magnetic draw, I went. There were volunteers in back who gave us Bibles and a note card to fill out and explained again what had just happened.

I was in a group of about 10 people and the person leading our group explained things one more time. He shared about how according to the Bible, everyone is a sinner because we have missed God's mark, the 10 Commandments. The Bible says if you have broken one commandment once you're guilty of breaking them all in

God's eyes. Uh oh - I was in trouble! But then he shared the good news part of it. He said that the Bible says, "the free gift of God is eternal life in Christ Jesus our Lord." He talked about Christmas gifts and how we can give a gift away and asked when it becomes the other person's gift - when we give it or when they accept it? He said it's the same thing as Christmas...that God is offering me a "free gift" of Heaven, and I need to make the conscious choice to accept that gift. He prayed with us one more time and then we left. The concert was over by the time we got out of the room. I was bummed! What I appreciated most about the entire evening was after the concert. Buddy was following up in the car asking if I knew what had just happened, etc. We went to the fast food restaurant where we worked, and Buddy urged me to tell the crew what had happened. I was reluctant at first but that quickly changed. I told the server "tonight I accepted Christ. I became a Christian."

Who knew what had happened would set my life on a new trajectory and save me - most literally - when things got crazy? The first seed of healing was planted that day. It might have taken a while to germinate, but the seed was planted. And boy did it start taking off!

I was home for the rest of the summer. I was working and playing on a church softball league. Through that league, I met a couple ladies who would quickly become friends. Sue and Ronda attended a nearby church and as we started to hang out at softball, they invited me to attend their Wednesday evening young adult group. Mom and Dad were cool with it so long as I still attended Catholic Mass with the family on Sunday. Attending Sue and Ronda's church was an eye-opening experience. I had never attended a non-Catholic church service, so it took some getting used to, but it quickly grew on me. By the time I had to go back for my senior year of college I considered Philadelphia Church of God my second church.

When I returned to campus in the Fall, I hit the ground running. What was sad, though, is that my lifestyle hadn't changed. I may have said I became a Christian over the summer, but you couldn't really tell from my actions. Turns out it took a year for me to realize my lifestyle was supposed to change. I had come to Christ and a lot of seeds had been planted leading up to that night. I just didn't have any real connections to share with at school. I was in a sorority, ran track, and was just focusing on enjoying - and finishing - my senior year of college.

I did it...I finished my senior year and graduated. Graduation day was a happy-sad day. I had accepted an opportunity to interview for two graduate assistantships at Mankato State University the week after graduation. My parents drove me three hours home from college on Sunday after graduation long enough to unpack and repack and get back in the car headed to Minnesota. I had to be there Tuesday night. I had one interview Tuesday night and the other on Wednesday. That was on my mind while having to say goodbye to Ed. He had played such a major role in me even GETTING to graduation that I found it very hard to say goodbye. I knew "He who began a good work in (me) will complete it until the day of Christ Jesus." (Phil. 1:6). I just didn't realize it was happening yet.

My Uncle Bill and Aunt Audrey had come to graduation and had given me a Catholic Bible as a graduation gift. The difference between a Catholic Bible and any other mainstream Bible is the Catholic Bible has a few extra books in it that aren't looked to as part of the original 66 books by all other denominations. At that moment, I didn't really know the difference...or care. I found myself drawn to it. I went through my "can't get enough" syndrome where I was devouring an epistle a night. I clearly remember sitting on my bed before going to sleep and reading an entire epistle (in the New Testament) a night and highlighting the daylights out of the pages. There was an insatiable hunger to read the Bible, something that had never happened in all my years of Catholic school or CCD. I now see that God was laying the foundation for things that were about to happen at grad school.

This much I know...God loves us and desires to have a relationship with us so much that He will use any means to draw us...even music.

Chapter 5

The Adventure Begins

It was Spring 1986, a few months before graduation. I was still deciding what to do after graduation. I had wanted to be a high school teacher and eventually move up to teach college, but because I did the usual college thing and changed my major four times, it would take one more semester for me to finish my teaching certificate. This was at a time when taking more than four years to finish college was more unusual. It made it seem something was wrong with you - kind of like getting held back in grade school. I had an interview and job offer from Kinney Shoe Stores to be an Assistant Manager. And then walking through the hall of the guys' residence hall one day I saw a poster with a tear-off postcard for graduate assistantships in Residential Life at Mankato State University in Minnesota. Now the only "Mankato" I knew of was from Little House on the Prairie, a popular TV show at that time. I sent in the card and within a couple weeks had an information packet.

I had been over-involved in campus activities so as I read through the information, I thought I could possibly qualify for an assistantship. I completed the application, sent it in, and waited. Now at the sorority house each person had a memo board on her room door for messages. But realize, long before cell phones and email, there was one phone in the middle of the hallway next to the community bathroom. It was one phone for 15 people, so you were at the mercy of someone answering the phone and taking a message for you, and hopefully getting the message right! I came back one day to a cryptic message on my white board, barely recognizable. It took a good amount of mental energy to recognize the name, and even then, I had to do a little asking around for who took the message.

Turns out it was Jerry Olson from Mankato State University inviting me to campus to interview for an assistantship!!!! The ballgame suddenly changed! Not only was I about to be the first child in my family to GRADUATE college, but I was now being recruited for graduate school!

I called Mom and Dad and was bubbling with excitement. They were equally excited and agreed to drive me the 1,500 miles from Dayton, Ohio to Mankato, Minnesota. I graduated on a Sunday and afterwards we drove home to Dayton. We left that Monday for the two-day trip to the university. We got as far as Rochester, Minnesota the first day and visited my cousin who is also the godchild of my mom and dad. We made the last couple hour trek on Tuesday afternoon and my first interview was Tuesday night. You see, as it just so happened, the application I submitted was sent to ALL student services departments, so I had also received a call from Scott Hagenboom in Student Activities, also inviting me to interview for a graduate assistantship. It was certainly one stop shopping! So, I had my interview with Student Activities on Tuesday and Residential Life on Wednesday. And that's where things got to be interesting.

We hit campus and had a couple hours before I was picked up for the interview. They gave us housing in a guest apartment in one of the towers on the far side of campus. The interview itself went well. They didn't do the campus tour or anything since I would get that the next day. On the way back from the Student Union, I had an experience like never before. Mind you, I had only been a believer in Christ about a year so this whole "hearing from God" thing was a foreign language to me.

I remember walking the couple blocks across campus back to the guest apartment when three sentences came to mind. They were not audible, but I heard God. Clear as day. Unmistakable. Distinct. His message to me was simply this: "I want you here for a reason. Don't ask why. Just trust Me." OK then!

My interview with Residential Life went equally well the next day. We enjoyed a two-day trip back to Ohio where I started my regular summer job and waited for the phone to ring. I was told they hoped to have an answer by the Tuesday or Wednesday following my interviews. I tried hard not to get my hopes up too high. I had no other clue what I would do if this didn't work out. I had made no other plans. I guess I had unknowingly put all my eggs in one basket.

I believe it was a Tuesday late afternoon when the phone rang - you know, the old old-style phones that were mounted to the wall and had a long handset cord so you could go outside for privacy if you slammed the cord in the door. Mom answered, asked the caller to hold, and said "Sue, it's Scott from Mankato State. He doesn't sound too excited." I replied, "That's just Scott."

The next two minutes on the phone were ones that would again change the trajectory of my life in yet unknown ways. Scott again thanked me for coming to interview, said they had discussed my application, and that the Student Activities Office was offering me a Graduate Assistantship in their office! It included a stipend and paid tuition. Mom and Dad and whichever siblings were home were all hanging on every word of the one-ended conversation they could hear. I was trying so hard just to keep it together, sound professional, and not squeal like a little girl! I calmly explained that I was also expecting to hear from Residential Life the same day, and I'd like to hear from them first before making any decision. Scott fully understood that and asked that I call him back the next day.

I hung up the phone. My face was beaming like a full moon at midnight with a clear sky. Tears began to fill my eyes and the smile broke out from ear to ear. Mom, Dad and siblings waited patiently with large, hope-filled eyes, thinking they knew the answer but waiting for the blanks to be filled. I leaned against the sink, blurrily looked at everyone, and simply said with a tone of disbelief, "I'm going to graduate school!'

Joy broke out in the kitchen that day. This was unchartered territory for anyone in our family. I was already a trailblazer simply by graduating college, but to even CONSIDER the next step was as huge as Columbus crossing the ocean! All along I really had no clue what I was doing. It was, quite frankly, an impulsive or impromptu decision even to send for more information in the first place. I had sought input from my Dean of Students (Joel Daniels) because I wasn't even sure what a degree in College Student Services was all about. All I knew was I was deeply involved in student activities at my college, loved every minute of it, and thought it would be cool to continue working in a field I never knew, until the last couple of months, even existed! Who knew that there were degree programs to become a Dean of Students or a Residence Hall Director or a Student Activities Director!

Sure enough, an hour or so later the phone rang again. This time it was Jerry Olson. It didn't take long for Jerry to offer me a graduate assistantship in Residential Life. Now I was confused! Ecstatic, but confused. I explained to him that Student Activities had also offered a position, and I needed time to think about it. Mom and Dad were so proud. I think all of us were beyond words.

All that night, I was thinking and processing, and Mom and Dad just listened. But they also said the decision had to be mine. They suggested I call my Dean of Students the next morning. I did just that. As it turns out, Joel knew Jerry. Small world. Joel and I had a great conversation. He said a lot of people get their start in the field through Residential Life, as he did. As I continued to think, I also got practical. The Res Life position included an apartment AND a stipend and 24 free meals a quarter. I've always been practical, even when I didn't realize that's what I was doing. But let's think about this -- Minnesota. In the winter. Living off campus. With no car. Hmmm...shoot, I didn't even get my license until right before I left for grad school!

In the end, I accepted the Residential Life graduate assistantship position...not just for practicality's sake, but also because I had a lot of background experience in Student Activities and wanted something new. If this was going to be my chosen career, then I wanted to start working on my resume` now! When I made my call to Jerry, he was obviously pleased but also indicated they knew that Student Activities was going to offer, just as Student Activities knew Residential Life was going to offer. It's nice to be wanted!

And so began this began a crazy two-year chapter in my life. In just a few months, I had gone from telling someone about the rape for the first time in my life, to graduating college, applying to one graduate school in the country, being accepted, and interviewing for two graduate assistantships, being offered both! My head was spinning JUST a little bit! And I had no idea God was just getting started!

I arrived on campus at the beginning of August. We Hall Directors had to report a few weeks before the students arrived so we could go through training and prepare for the arrival of our residence hall staffs and conduct their training. I had never been an RA in college and was certainly figuring this thing out on the fly.

I made it through all of staff training and found myself starting my grad school classes. I say I was slow out of the starting gate. Others were meeting with their advisors on a regular basis, and I was getting involved in college groups like I did in undergrad! I found my way to the Newman Center, the Catholic faith representation on campus. I started hanging out at the Newman House and talking with Father Joe and Sister Joyce, attending the campouts, and singing in the guitar group at church. Through the course of my involvement, I met Steve Breiter.

I heard music coming from down the hallway. Someone had a tape in (long before CDs and MP3 files ever existed) and the piano music was beautiful. I asked what he was listening to and Steve replied that he was listening to a Michael W. Smith tape and liked the instrumental stuff that was included at the end of the tape. I was still new to Christianity but was enjoying listening to some good music.

A few doors down the hall from my apartment, I heard other music. This was a little rockier but with still powerful lyrics. I met Mike Carney and he was playing Petra. Curious! I remember that band! Between Steve and Mike, I started having conversations about Christian music and began to be exposed to more of it. I liked it. The more I listened to it, I also started listening to a Christian music station I could get in my apartment. Little did I know how much this exposure was going to influence my life.

By the time spring quarter had rolled around, some things started to change. Mike Carney, my friend and resident, had left school for an internship in the Twin Cities. I then received word that he had been killed in an accident while biking to work. I was crushed. Mike had become special to me, and we were able to have a lot of conversations. He really helped me start out on my Christian walk. Emotionally, it started to take a toll. On top of that, my parents were struggling in their marriage and were probably headed for divorce. I was hurting and didn't know how to handle it. Grad school stress was starting to hit as I had to apply to the program and only had one more quarter to get the necessary grades. I was withdrawing socially and becoming a little desperate...desperate for an outlet, for someone to care and for someone with whom I could talk. As it would later turn out, that turning point, once again, came at a Christian concert.

I had heard about a Christian rock concert by an artist named Rick Cua. I wasn't familiar with his music, but something drew me. I rented a car and headed to the Twin Cities on what amounted to my first solo out-of-town excursion. I found the church and lurked in the back row, yearning for something and not sure what it was or how to ask for it. The concert was enjoyable, and at the end, Rick led the audience in a prayer of dedication or rededication to Christ. I prayed the prayer and even went forward at the end of the concert to let someone else pray with me and receive a Bible. It was my first "real" Bible since I came to Christ. Remember, the only other Bible I had ever received was a Catholic Bible, the previous year when I graduated college.

Rick was signing autographs, and I shyly approached him, waiting until a good portion of the crowd had left. He recognized my Bible as one they were giving away and asked about the decision I made that night. It was good to talk a bit. He was very encouraging and seemed genuinely attentive and concerned. I left feeling more settled, a little more peaceful, and certainly more hopeful. What I didn't know is what God was starting to do through that night.

Something changed in me over the summer. I was taking a summer class (Stats - UGH!) and working conferences on campus and listening to Christian music, enjoying it more and more. I attended concerts when I could, but I decided to take it a step further my second year of grad school.

I was growing in my faith and feeling more energy and focus. And then I got this crazy idea. I started wondering what it would take to bring a Christian concert to campus. So, I did what any other second year grad school student writing a master's paper and taking classes, while interviewing for jobs and studying for comps would do: I spearheaded bringing Rick Cua to campus for a concert! I never claimed to be wise!

Looking back, I honestly don't know how we pulled it off. The group helping me brought him in through a campus organization and did a bunch of promotional stuff. I remember walking a few miles to the Christian bookstore on the edge of town to hang up posters and arrange an in-store appearance for Rick. We had all kinds of promo up on campus. We were ready.

The concert itself took place in the last month or so of school and was a success. For me, it took place the night before my comps, or comprehensive exams. Comps are a four-hour essay exam covering everything learned in grad school. It's graded Pass or Fail. Period.

And instead of staying home to rest or review, I was running a concert! Like I said, I never claimed to be wise! In my defense, the concert contract was signed long before my comps were scheduled.

This was my first "concert event" to promote, and I just flew by the seat of my pants. But it worked! I have since learned that God has gifted me with being able to put together large events in quick fashion. It sounds crazy to some, but in five minutes I can create a list of what is needed to pull off an event. I just didn't know it until now. Remember Tanya Crevier, the basketball handler who came to my undergraduate college to perform her show? I had brought Tanya to perform on campus during the winter. And then it was Rick. I guess you can say I was an "atypical" grad student in that I got involved in the campus activities and student groups and took the helm to do some campus-wide programming through the groups. What I didn't realize was God was just getting started!

God laid the foundation and got a hold of my heart in a fresh way during my time in Minnesota. Especially through the event promotions, I realized I could continue booking Christian talent to perform on campus. My relationships with performers took root during my time at Mankato. I began attending more Christian concerts during my two years there. I saw Michael W. Smith for the first time. I greatly value telling people how they have affected my life, and I began to write some of the musicians and other friends to do just that. I never would have guessed where this would lead in the years to come!

I said I was a slow starter in grad school. It took a while for me to catch on and figure out things. And as weird as it may sound, I enjoyed writing my master's paper. My second chapter - the review of the literature which is usually the longest chapter - only had one re-write on it. I was proud that although there were six folks in my program, only two of us finished our papers in time to be considered "May graduates," and I was one of them! I learned so much in grad school and even more about life outside of the classroom. So many of the things and decisions made in those two pivotal years of my life set my life on a crazy path that can only be described as a "But God" experience!

This much I know... following God, even when you don't realize you're doing it, leads to one great adventure.

Chapter 6

Coming Out of the Dark

It wasn't that long into the Fall Quarter at Mankato when something started happening within me. Remember my secret I shared with Ed at Defiance earlier in the year? Well, as it would have it, secrets have a way of leaking out once the cover is cracked.

Amy Ginther was my ACD (Associate Complex Director). She supervised the entire residence complex, where I supervised one wing of it. In short, Amy was my boss. And she was cool!

Amy was easy-going, available, visible, knowledgeable, fun and encouraging. She was well-respected by the entire building, knew how to have fun, and was just very "real" with us. She even shared stories of Gus her cat! I was the new kid on the block, certainly felt a little behind the crowd, and uncertain but willing to learn. There was one night that totally changed the trajectory of not only my time at MSU, but in essence my entire life. I just didn't know it at that time.

The quarter was off and rolling. Amy would be found a couple nights a week working later in her office. There was one night where I was headed down to the front desk for whatever reason and saw Amy in her office. I stopped by to talk with her as I was struggling. I don't remember the details, but in the course of the conversation she could tell something was bothering me. She had already seen me through a back issue that happened while on staff retreat at a Girl Scout camp. For three days, I was stiff and barely able to turn to my head. She checked on me daily and had said, "If you're not better by tomorrow I'm taking you to a chiropractor." That night I sat on the floor against a recliner because that was most comfortable....and sure enough I heard my back crack 3-4 times and my neck loosened.

Amy was good at reading people, so as we talked, she could tell something was on my mind. She just calmly asked about what was on my mind. I couldn't look her in the eye. Up until this moment, what was about to escape from my lips had only been murmured twice. It wasn't something I was ready to talk about, but it wanted to come out anyway. Slowly, quietly, tearfully, the words leaked out. I told Amy what I had told Ed a few months earlier. I told Amy I had been raped as a child.

Her response was priceless. Compassionate. Concerned, Heartbroken. She gave me tissues, asked a few questions, and gave me a reassuring touch. Then she asked something that I think I had wanted but didn't know how to ask for. She suggested I talk with a counselor at the University Counseling Office and asked if she could make a call to set up an appointment. She offered to go with me. I agreed. A little wave of relief swept over me as the tears cascaded. Maybe, just maybe, this would be the start I was secretly wanting but didn't know how to ask for, and I would find some relief from my 15-year secret.

My phone rang the next day. It was Amy. She had an appointment set with Sandy Hyde at the Counseling Center. I was to meet Amy at the office at an agreed upon time and she would go with me, at least long enough to introduce me to Sandy.

The time came to meet Amy. I remember feeling as if in a daze on the way to her office. She was pleasant, sensitive, supportive and concerned. We walked across the campus to the 2nd floor of the Student Union where the Counseling Office was located. I remember feeling so conspicuous and nervous about what others would think. Amy checked us in...and we waited. It wasn't long, but it felt like an eternity. I'm not sure if I made eye contact with Amy or not. We chatted and she did her best to reassure me. I was still nervous. I don't know anyone who wouldn't have been. And then I heard it... a soft female voice.

"Sue?"

Amy and I stood up. There was no turning back now.

We went to Sandy's office, and the three of us sat. Amy took the lead to try to break the ice. She told Sandy there was something I had told her, and that I agreed to talk with Sandy about it. The three of us talked a few more minutes and as things settled, Amy excused herself with the instruction to see her when I got back. Then Amy left. And I was left alone in the office to start sharing my story.

It took a little doing but in the course of that first appointment I told Sandy what happened......... I told her about being raped by Bobby when I was 7 years old. What I didn't know, is the springboard this would become for my future healing. We talked for that entire hour, and she asked if I was willing to come back. That part was a no-brainer. I had tried keeping it a secret for 15 years. It was slowly eating me alive and I had made my first choice: healing. In this case, it meant making another appointment to keep opening a gangrenous wound that was far exceeding my 15-year band aid.

When I left Sandy's office, I returned to the residence hall. I was shaking and avoiding eye contact, feeling as if the whole world suddenly knew my secret. It was the same feeling I had at Defiance after telling Ed. I went to the front desk and inside my mailbox was a note from Amy. It simply read: "Sue: You made my day. I'm proud of you. Come have a muffin." I went back to Amy's office and a smile lit her face when she saw me. I sat down, she closed the door, she offered a muffin, and we talked. And that made it safe to share my story, safe to ask for help, and safe to be afraid.

It would be a long two years sitting in Sandy's office every week having some tough conversations! We did the MMPI (Minnesota Multiphasic Personality Inventory) and dug where I had never dug before. We didn't heal everything in two years. I wish! But we got the ball rolling. Sandy recommended I continue counseling with someone when I started my first job after graduation. She knew I had a long way to go. But the journey started, all because Amy was in her office and available. And oh - the muffins were great too!

It was all still new to me and though I had told my secret about being raped, I still didn't know what that really meant in terms of having to feel all my emotions before the wounds could begin to heal. Saying the words versus doing the hard work to heal are two VERY different things! And no one had told me how long and painful the healing and recovery process would take. Nonetheless, I had started on this journey, not knowing where it will lead or what it would cost me.

This much I know...God shows Himself through the little things...muffins, a listening ear, a hand to hold, a hug to give, a walk together to an office to alleviate the fear. He will show Himself in whatever way is needed to meet the need in the heart of the person for whom He seeks.

Chapter 7

Escape to the Woods

Remember those three sentences that came to mind when I was interviewing for graduate assistantships? "I want you here for a reason. Don't ask why. Just trust me." While I had no idea then what door was starting to open for me, looking back now it makes total sense.

One day I came back from class and checked my mail like usual. In my box was a magazine to which I had not subscribed: Prime Time Magazine. It featured a lot of well-known Christian musicians and athletes. I had just started listening to more Christian music, as I had only been a believer a year. I received a total of four magazines and enjoyed each one. The person putting them out was a gentleman named Joe White who lived in Branson, Missouri. I don't remember what it was, but something at some point made me want to write him. I liked what I saw in the magazines and he just seemed like a cool guy. What I didn't know then was that a long-standing friendship was about to develop - one that remains to this day.

It was a crazy enough idea to write a guy I had never met, but imagine my shock when I received a return letter! And it was personal! And he signed it too! Thus, a two- year pen-pal friendship with Joe began.

After graduating with my Master of Science degree, I spent the summer at home before starting my first job at Hanover College in Hanover, Indiana. I was to be an Assistant Dean of Students - their title for a residence hall director. I also had some responsibility with Student Activities.

That year was an interesting one. The fit with the job itself was not a good one but finding the Fellowship of Christian Athletes (FCA) group and being asked to serve as their advisor was the highlight of the year. The group's numbers grew, sponsored a Steve Camp concert, attended the Midwest Regional Retreat in western Indiana, and a couple special friendships grew. The FCA President, Jeff Foutty, became one of those students with whom I just really hit it off. Jeff would visit me at my office and just talk - life, Christianity, the group. We just really enjoyed talking with each other, so when I knew I would not be returning to the campus the following year it was hard to say goodbye.

It was after spring break and we were headed to the Midwest Regional FCA Retreat. I had just recently learned my contract would not be renewed for the following year. Rich Mullins's project "Winds of Heaven...Stuff of Earth" had just come out, and one song, in particular, was very poignant for me: "Ready for the Storm." I listened to the album on the three-hour drive across the state and on the way back. There was something that resonated with me in the lyrics. I think it was the sentiment that no matter what storm is happening (unemployment), there is no reason to be frightened when He is in the boat.

Those magazines I received in grad school ended up having a more important part to play around this time. I had ordered the paperback books written by Joe White, the Director of Kanakuk Kamps, and had been finding myself thinking "those kamps sound like a lot of fun. I wonder what it'd be like to work there." After finding out I needed to find a new job I did the usual thing - updated my resume and made plans to attend a professional conference to interview at the job fair...and I wrote Kanakuk asking for an application. It was only my first year post graduate, so I had no idea what Student Services professionals did during the summers...so I was winging it! I had a phone interview and before I knew it, I was offered the Dining Hall Discipleship position at K-2, THE kamp where Joe White was stationed! I accepted, packed my bags, stopped at home for a couple days and then flew out to Missouri, not knowing what was ahead of me but knowing Who was navigating my journey through the storm.

From the minute I stepped into the Kamp, there was something very different about that place. Staff Week was a lot of work but a lot of fun. However, being in a frame of mind that was fragile and guarded from my past, I didn't know how to be around all that love, not to mention accept it! I didn't see myself as loveable. It was good enough for everyone else but not for me. I specifically remember being at a chapel service before the Kampers arrived and approaching Joe after he was done speaking. I shyly commented to him, "I'm finding myself withdrawing from everything. I don't know how to accept the love." Joe took out his thinline New Testament with his name engraved on it and told me "Try. Try to take this." I tried and it wasn't going anywhere because Joe was still holding it tightly. Then he looked at me and said, "Trying gets you nowhere. Now take it." He let go of his grasp and released the Bible, and I was able to easily take it from his hand. Joe's next words have stayed with me since: "Accept the love the same way you accepted Christ. Don't ask why, just say thanks."

It turns out accepting love would be the lesson I learned during the five summers I spent in the Ozarks, not knowing at the time it was laying the groundwork for what God wanted to do within me decades later. I called my time at Kamp my "summer escape to the woods." You would not find this place on a Sunday drive without the road signs. Every summer, for five years, I packed my bags at the end of May and headed west - 730 miles one-way to be exact. Some years I left by 6:30a.m. and landed at Kamp right around dinner time. Other years, I made it a two-day trek and got to Kamp just after breakfast. Either way, I knew where I was going and couldn't wait to get there. Those ten weeks every year were my respite. Mom and Dad were divorcing, I was hurting, confused, scared, and lonely, and Kanakuk gave me a chance to get away from the pressure and just refocus. I never went to church camp when I was growing up, but I sure loved Kamp.

Friendships were founded at Kamp that held a depth unknown to me anywhere else. Some folks I met at Kamp I am still friends with today. I had many life adventures at Kamp - rappelling, learning to swim, jumping off the faith poles 20 feet in the air and reaching for a trapeze, riding a horse, wind-surfing, tubing, attempting to water ski.....if there is one thing Kamp does, it brings people out of their shyness. Mom told me every year, "Don't tell me what you do until you get home." I've never been one for costume parties. I always felt stupid and rarely had a good costume, yet Kamp had three parties every term, and the kids went all out on their costumes! We would dance and play games and just have fun. It was so much fun watching teenagers be uninhibited in their costumes and party themes. It really challenged me to not overthink things and not be concerned about what others thought. I wouldn't realize until recently all those inhibitions and fears were my eating disorder taking charge.

What's funny is that the thing I value most from my time at Kamp was serving. I was on the kitchen staff. We served 400 people, three meals a day, in a non-air-conditioned kitchen, where the dish sanitizer machine (affectionately named Hobie after its brand name) would reach 140 degrees Fahrenheit from the steam. We fed Fred, which was the name of the never seen pig the local farmers fed with the table scrapings from Kamp. Imagine a 33-gallon trash can - or more like four of them - put in one room with a screen door entrance. At the end of each meal, the pots of plate scrapings from all the tables would get dumped into one of the trash cans where it would sit...and get warm in the hot Ozark weather...and continue to have more added to it until the farmers came to pick up the trash cans. Yeah, it took a big sense of humor to "feed Fred." It took an even bigger sense of humor to go CLEAN Fred...as in remove the cans and clean out the room where they were kept, complete with a bleach wipe down. After all, there were JUST a few flies around the mountains too!

We made it fun. Attitude is everything, and while the kids and counselors might be having a bad day, time and time again we heard how much they loved coming to the dining hall, not only to eat, but because we made it fun. We might set the table for them, or make some table decorations, or anything else we could do to make it special and homey. I learned that serving is a lot of fun regardless of what anyone else may think, because serving gets our eyes off ourselves. At Kamp, I finally found a place to belong, where I felt I mattered, where I felt loved and accepted. For the first time in my life, I felt like I had an identity.

During the school year, Kamp would recruit staff for the next summer. There would be a compilation video made and teams of full time Kamp Staff would travel the country to reunite with kampers, and staff alike, while recruiting and interviewing for the following summer's staff. It was called "Movie Tour," and the closest it would come to Ohio was Nashville, Tennessee. I made it my purpose every fall to drive to Nashville for a weekend, get a hotel room, and stay for Kamp movies on Saturday night and return to Ohio after church on Sunday. I also used the time to visit with my Kamp friends.

Joe White is well known and travels the world speaking with Promise Keepers, Focus on the Family, and other organizations. When Joe was producing the Today's Prime Time Magazine I received in graduate school, he got to know several well-known Christian musicians. Many of these musicians would visit Kamp or send their kids to Kamp, and it was not uncommon to hear the comment, "You may see some folks you recognize today. They are here as family and not stars, so no pictures, no autographs. This is their chance to just be normal, and it's how we love them when they are here." Some of these people would visit Kamp during a term to do a concert, and I was blessed to get to know some of them through Kamp and other avenues. Going to Nashville also gave me opportunity to visit with my musician friends. I always told them, "I don't care how you pay your bills. I want to know your heart." Some of those people are friends still today, and while they are very normal in my eyes, I never take for granted the gift God has given in getting to know them. Even today, some of these people are friends my family and I get to see when they are on tour. Just another blessing for the future from my time at Kanakuk.

One key moment in my life happened at a Discipleship Ski trip Kanakuk sponsored. We had done a gut-wrenching intervention on my Dad in 1990, and Mom and Dad were divorcing. I felt caught in the middle, and I shut down. My emotions were frozen. I was starting to drink again, and my eating disorder was in full operation. I was at an unhealthy weight.

Billy Sprague was one of my musician friends from Kanakuk. His fiancé had been killed in an automobile accident on her way to surprise Billy at a concert. Billy found out right before going on stage. He was neck deep in grief and over time became suicidal from the grief. We had lost touch but reconnected before the trip.

It was the last day of the trip. I had asked to talk with Billy, so he and I stayed at the lodge after the others left for the slopes.

"So, what's up?", Billy asked.

"I need to learn from something you've gone through. My question for you is this: how do you go on living when ALL you want to do is die?"

"What's going on?"

For the next 90 minutes Billy and I talked. When we were done, Billy said "That's all I know to tell you Sue. Step by step."

Billy had shared that during his struggle he had gone to watching his shoes, telling himself with each step, "One step closer." He had me watch my boots on the way to the slopes. The first thought I had was, "God, it's a long journey, and I'm not going to make it." I'm glad I was wrong. It took six months for my heart to begin to thaw after the divorce, but it thawed. I have Billy to thank for helping me through, and I am grateful to have had the opportunity to tell him that several times over the years.

I was searching for belonging, an identity, acceptance, and love. I found it at Kanakuk, not knowing what God was doing through it.

This much I know...God's lessons can meet the same needs decades apart.

Chapter 8

A Good Thing Gone Bad

After I left Hanover, I started working at Ohio Wesleyan University (OWU). It is in Delaware, Ohio, about 20 miles north of Columbus, so entertainment was easy to find. My favorite past time was to attend Christian concerts, especially at a place called The King's Place. They tended to book some of the artists who were newer and still building their fan base, as it was the late 80s and early 90s and Christian music was taking off. While I saw a few artists there and even volunteered there at times, one concert in particular started me down a path, which was good and bad. As is often the case with God, I just didn't know it at the time.

I attended a Margaret Becker concert. Margaret was really the first female Christian artist in the rock genre who also played electric guitar. She was an industry breath of fresh air at the time. As the venue was small and the artists were still newer, they often came out to sign autographs after the show. I waited to see her and got into a small conversation with a couple folks in front of me. What I didn't know is where that would lead.

A week or two later at an OWU football game I saw someone at the stadium who was wearing the same shirt as I: a Margaret Becker concert shirt. We struck up a conversation and I was asked where I went to church. I told her I was doing "the great search" for a new church and was immediately invited to her church. It was on the east side of Columbus which made it about a 30-minute drive for me, but when you're searching you'll go wherever you can find something.

The following week I visited the church which, at that time, met at a middle school. The folks were friendly though I was guarded. It was different than anything I had been a part of up to that point in my life. Remember, I had been raised Catholic so anything outside of a formal liturgy was almost "foreign" to me. I made it through the service and there was something about it which drew me, intrigued me, and left me thinking about it. I was asked if I would return the following week and I shyly said "probably." I returned the following week, and the week after...and before I knew it, I had found a permanent church.

For the first year or so, I attended but wasn't involved in any other way. I knew a couple folks, watched them play soccer, and hung out at their place at times. Over time my friendship with Judy grew and she would call me spontaneously to see if I wanted to play Trivial Pursuit at her place. One night at 11p, I traveled the 25 minutes to her place, and we went to Meijer to buy new cards, and played the game until 1 or 2am, eating snacks and drinking Yoohoo! all night. It felt great to have a friend and have a social life! Even with all that, though, I wasn't really connected. But something kept me going back to the church each week. I was a young believer and had at least found a little fellowship while I was figuring out this Christianity thing.

The distance was always in the back of my mind. The church was part of something called the Great Commission Association of Churches. I had never heard of it before. After I had been there for about a year, the church had purchased some property about 20 minutes from where they had been meeting. I remember the first service at the new property. It was about five minutes longer than the current drive. As I found my way to a side of Columbus, OH I only knew for concerts, I remember thinking "This is too far. I can't keep doing this." To this day I can't tell you what the pastor, Mike Keator, spoke about that day, but I left there saying, "I don't care how far it is. I'm not leaving." At that point it became a priority to get involved.

I became involved in numerous ways with the church - sound tech, youth leader, drama ministry co-director, worship team, and eventually Office Manager. I got involved in small groups and enjoyed being there any chance I could. Before I was on staff I would volunteer at the office when I had a day off work. Because I had a strong need to be liked and accepted, I wasn't sharp enough to see some of the things going on which ended up being very wrong and damaging. I guess I noticed it in hindsight but didn't know better to question it. You see, I had only been a believer for four years when I stumbled across Great Commission. I had never been "discipled" or had anyone help me learn what it means to be a Christian and figure out how to live the way Christ desires. I was figuring it out on my own, so I was hungry, a sponge, letting anything that resembled water pour on me. Looking back, I see things more clearly than when it was happening, but there were some unhealthy things happening. There were a lot of good things, too, and those good things made it harder to see the other things.

The church was serious about making disciples. There were classes on spiritual growth, discipleship groups, Bible studies. There were opportunities to learn how to share the gospel by going to Ohio State's campus and learning how to do a spiritual interest survey which could lead to sharing the gospel with someone. It was there that I first learned how to share the gospel. To say I was nervous was an understatement. I felt stupid to be honest. My inner voices were whispering how inept I was, how unskilled I was, how much Chuck, the associate pastor training me, would judge me. I was really only doing this because I just wanted to be seen. I was insecure, and one thing I was starting to realize is that if you got "trained" and if you got in the "in" crowd you were looked at as a potential leader. And if I was a leader I would be "seen" even more and maybe, just maybe, I would feel like I amounted to something, like I had worth, like I had value. Even in college I always associated my "worth" with my activities and unfortunately it carried over to my church involvement. Sadly, it worked.

I quickly went from a fringe member to a youth leader. I left Ohio Wesleyan after five years to go on staff with GCM, the missionary arm of the church association. I worked in the national headquarters office helping coordinate conferences, especially the teens. I was doing national high school ministry. But before I got to that point, I went through a lot. And somehow survived.

In my years as a youth leader, I came to understand the "pecking order" of ministry leadership. Because I was a woman, and single, in the eyes of the association, I was not "qualified" to be the "ministry leader" but only an assistant. You see, this association firmly believed that the leadership of church ministries was to be led by men. Women could assist but could not be the "point person" unless it was a children's or women's ministry. Not knowing better, I bought in. At every point in time over the years, I was "under" a couple leading the youth ministry. I felt like a cog in the wheel, second fiddle, and that I couldn't be free to use my gifts. No matter what I tried, there just wasn't connection. No matter what happened, I just felt like the odd man (woman) out.

The best way to describe the big issue is a wrong submission to authority. Don't get me wrong - we are to submit to authority if we are not being asked to do anything illegal, immoral, or unethical. But this had to do with an unspoken attitude of doing what your pastors "counseled" you to do and if you didn't you were being "disobedient." It was about control. You see, there's nothing wrong with getting counsel from a spiritual leader on matters where you desire input. We're SUPPOSED to do that! But when that "counsel" becomes "commandment" it has crossed the line, and wherever the attitude of "counsel is directive" developed - and wasn't stopped by the leaders - I don't know, but it was wrong. I felt it as a "newbie." I heard people - especially singles - talk about "well ___ said I should do ___" and they blindly followed. Little room was given for individual decision making or trusting a person to follow Christ's lead. It was as if the pastors had the corner market on what God says in how to handle something so there was no need to think or pray about it yourself to make your own decision...to discern for yourself while taking into consideration the input from the pastors.

I fell into it. I wanted to be accepted by the pastors and looked to as a leader and not a "project to be fixed." I wanted them to see me as someone who was committed to following Christ and would do anything to prove it. Right there is a red flag, but I was too young in my faith to see it. Thankfully, in my situation, it wasn't manipulated, but there was one specific area where harm was done: being single.

It was the viewpoint of this organization, from my experience, that the "ideal" was to be married, have kids, and homeschool them as a stay-at-home mom, and if not, then being single was okay but you should be knit into a family to see what having a family looked like as "preparation" for when you will be married. Being single, living alone, and having a career wasn't the best option. At the VERY least have a few roommates for community and accountability. Again, there is nothing wrong with those things when it is under the right atmosphere, but when the overriding attitude of the church is that it is best to be married, there's a problem. Singles were seen as "glorified babysitters", often under the guise of serving a family.

The first time it happened, our new assistant pastor called me asking if I would be willing to watch his kids while he and his wife went out. Now mind you, I was 45 minutes away! Yes, I was newer, and it was a good chance to get to know me a little, and in my naivete I jumped at it. I felt special. After all, he said I was the first person he thought of! It was a little awkward after they got home as I wasn't sure if I was supposed to ask for money or not. We talked a while and got to know each other and then I was free to go. And the babysitting was free. It was never discussed, just assumed. He and his family had been part of the organization for a long time so they "knew;" I did not. There was another time the church was having a daylong conference for couples and a number of the younger kids all hung out at the pastor's house for centralized childcare, and a number of singles were asked to help with the kids. Years later, when I moved in with a family, part of the rental agreement was, I would cook dinner for the kids once a week so the parents could go out on a date night. It was just part of the pervasive attitude: "being single = free childcare."

Now don't get me wrong - there was a singles group and we did some things together, but it was more of a social event group than anything else. Now when it came to the annual convention the singles tended to share rooms together which cut on the expense, and the convention was usually comprised of college aged students, campus staff, and singles. The couples usually didn't go to Convention, unless they were on staff or presenting.

Where this really screwed me up, looking back, is in working through issues of sexuality stemming from my rape. Anyone who has survived any kind of sexual assault knows the extreme affect it has, and recovery is having to face those issues and come to peace with them. Since my sense of sexuality was skewed from the start, and having been in a dysfunctional home environment with my parents' marriage ending in divorce, I never had opportunity to deal with issues of sexuality. Childhood trauma mixed with lack of healthy role models leads to more trauma and confusion.

It wasn't until 2018, when I began to realize everything I endured as spiritual abuse. I was angry about it. I was confused. I attended a new church which believes women can be lead pastors, and while that is a breath of fresh air, it is still something I am having to work through and resolve...all because a good thing went bad and scarred me as much as it helped me. It is interesting to run into people who used to attend the Great Commission Church I attended. Without fail, each one agrees it was wrought with spiritual abuse and control. While I was on staff there was a nasty church split and there is much I am taking to my grave...all because of the control issues and the "image" issues. It still leaves a bad taste in my mouth.

I have learned through all this that the struggles I had dealing with sexuality and my role in a relationship have been severely affected not only by the rape but also through the church teachings for the first 12 years I was a believer. Those were very foundational years and I am sad they had that poison as food for so long. I don't blame myself. Like any group with cult-like tendencies the control and the pervasive attitude of being unequal and unqualified is cloaked and disguised as "counsel" and "service." It has made me be more discerning, ask more questions, and be bold about something I don't understand, all the while being open about my experience so the context is understood. It took a long time to pull back this layer of the onion. It was hard to acknowledge the abuse and it often felt like another kick in the gut, but like everything else, the resilience brought me through, and I am wiser and better as a result.

This much I know...even when humans mess things up, God can still bring good!

Chapter 9

Amanda

One good thing that came from my time with Great Commission was my relationship with the Long family. While Chuck was the pastor who called me to watch his kids when I was 45 minutes away, he also said he was wanting to get me more involved with his family. The babysitting was just the start. Now yes, while the attitudes I shared about Great Commission were contributing to being invited to be involved with the Long family, as I said earlier, I was young and needy, so I jumped at the opportunity. It gave me a sense of belonging and connection since being 45 minutes away prohibited my involvement in many things. And hey - it was a pastor's family, so I knew I would be respected by others if I got "in" with a pastor's family!

Over time, my relationship with the Long's became very special. I would "hang out" with the kids and as they grew got a chance to tutor them once a week while Chuck and Melery were at a class at church. There were other times I would just go over to hang out and play with the kids. It gave me a break from my place and the kids enjoyed having someone to spend time with them. They called me "Miss Sue," and they helped me, too. Lindsay taught me to crochet so I could make a gift for my Compassion child I was going to meet in Honduras. I coached Parks and Rec soccer and the Longs were on my team and Chuck was my Asst. Coach once.

The underlying part of the relationship, however, was Chuck helping me. I was still screwed up and figuring out what it meant to be a believer and deal with my past, while struggling immensely in my present! Melery (like celery but with an M) was diagnosed with stage 4 breast cancer. She lived five plus years with it and met Jesus face-to-face on July 10, 2005. As a result, two of Chuck's daughters (they had seven kids) developed eating disorders and went to residential treatment in Arizona. As part of that process, Chuck met Amanda Washel, a Christian eating disorder counselor. Three years after Melery died, I met Amanda at Chuck's recommendation.

I had been out of counseling for a few years. Everything seemed to be going okay, and when I had things I was dealing with I talked with Chuck. He knew I had "anorexic tendencies," as I called them. I also knew my red flags, and about three years after Melery died, those red flags started going up again. One, is when I look in the refrigerator, get overwhelmed and can't decide what I want or can't find something fast, and shut it and just snack instead. That red flag was flying, as were others. I reached out to Chuck and told him, and he first suggested I contact Sandi Ridenour, my last counselor from almost a decade ago. I reached out to Sandi who, while remembering me, said she was not skilled in eating disorders to be able to get to the root. I followed up with Chuck who remembered Amanda and gave me her number.

Amanda and I talked on the phone at least three different times before my face ever walked through her door. She was SO easy to talk with and asked a lot of questions. All told, I think we talked close to 90 minutes before I made my first appointment. When we finally met, April 5, 2008, it was as if the ice had already been broken. I was broken at that point and wasn't sure if I could ever be put back together again. Yet early on, I also told Amanda, I wasn't going to quit until we were done because I wasn't going to go through this again. If I was going to do this, we were going to work through EVERYTHING! I asked her a few sessions in what she thought was causing the eating disorder to come back and she said, "I think it's just a bunch of unresolved issues." So, we got to work.

Every week, I drove 35 minutes to see Amanda. Saturday mornings at 8a were our time. We called it "The Breakfast Club." Some of those sessions were REALLY long ones and some flew by before we knew it. She is a master "digger" and we joke about how many "firsts" she has had with me. There was a chemistry and a connection from the start.

I never knew what to expect early on. I was so screwed up in the head that I was just trying to survive. She gave me homework each week, something I had never had from any other counselor. I actually liked it. I was desperate enough that I was willing to do whatever it took. My homework that first week was to do a life timeline - to write out every significant thing that had happened to me. Mine was four pages long, and it took about three sessions to get through it. I remember her starting to go through it in our second session. It started with winning my dog and Amanda said she had already had questions. We talked a minute, and then I told her it would come to a screeching halt when she got to the second item on the list. It was Bobby. She said something else and then stopped, saying she had looked ahead. She read what I wrote: "raped by Bobby Nolan - age 7." She looked at me as I inspected the weave of the carpet in her office and gently said, "Sue, this is HUGE! Did you ever work it through with anyone?" I just said, "I wouldn't know what it looked like to say I had worked it through, so I guess there's your answer." Needless to say, that made the list of things to be discussed at some point!

Amanda's favorite question early on was "how did that make you feel?" You see, folks who have eating disorders have figured a way to redirect emotions to behavior with food, and she was trying to get the brain jump started. I had to keep food journals and write what I ate, and how I was feeling when I ate it. Every little thing that went into my mouth, she wanted to know. Over the months of talking and beginning to thaw my heart, the emotions began to stir. But it was so much; I didn't know how to respond. It was December 22, 2008. I had only been working with her seven months. And one of my secrets came out.

I was struggling like nothing else. I was grieving Melery, and Chuck had resigned as pastor and moved to Colorado. I had made a choice to change churches, had just been laid off after being senior CSR at a company I worked at for almost nine years, and I was a mess. I had bought a pocketknife with about a 3-4" blade and one night in my room, when the pain was too great and needed a release, I made a mark on my arm. Not a big one. One that could be hidden. However, with enough pressure, it drew a little blood. I started cutting, though I wouldn't come to call it that for quite some time. I had already ended up telling Brian, my new pastor, when he checked on me. He wasn't happy, as I had lied to him about it 30 minutes earlier when he and I were talking. But Amanda didn't know.

She and I were talking and in the middle of it our conversation she just said, "I don't know why, but I really feel like I'm supposed to ask you this question. Have you thought about, or have you tried, to hurt yourself?"

"You HAD to ask that question, didn't you?" I replied.

"What happened Sue? What did you do?"

I sat on the couch for a minute, inspected my shoelaces and said, "I'll tell you the same way I told Brian," and I began to roll up the sleeve on my shirt. "These are what's left of marks I made on my arm."

Amanda tried to stay calm.

"Sue. We need to have a conversation. Do you need more help than we can give?"

I knew at that point I was talking for my life. I assured her it was okay (yeah, right), that I was fine, and that it was just marks on my arm, it wasn't cutting. How she kept from snickering is beyond me!

"What do you use?" she asked.

"A knife I bought."

"Where do you keep it?"

"I keep it with me."

"Do you have it with you now?"

"Yeah."

"May I see it?"

I pulled it from the pocket of my pants and handed it to her across the room. She looked at it, looked at me, and said "Sue, this isn't a knife. It's a weapon!"

We talked directly for the rest of the session. She had to be sure I wasn't going to hurt myself if she let me leave. In the end, we had an agreement in place. As she walked me to the door, she asked, "May I keep it? You'll get it back." I just looked at her and said, "You're going to keep it regardless." She smiled and reiterated, "You'll get it back." I dodged my first bullet with her and escaped as quickly as I could. Nevertheless, I confess I felt naked without my knife when I got to the car.

Thus began an amazing working relationship with Amanda. We talked, and we dug, and we kept at it. Numerous times I wanted to quit. At one point when I was tempted to pull out, she was on maternity leave and we were doing a phone session. As we talked, she asked me to commit to one more session with her before making any decision to which I said "There's no need for that. You and I both know what will happen if I quit, and I'm not starting over again. I'll be there for more than one more session."

Then there was the time I was losing weight. I believe it was the spring after the cutting issue. I had been seeing her almost a year, so by now the emotions were being pulled up, and we were dealing with a lot of present-day stuff. As she said, "We have to get you stronger in the present so we can deal with the past." My eating disorder behaviors were in full swing and I was NOT doing well. I was getting to a low weight - not my absolute lowest but headed in that direction - and she pulled no punches. She thought I needed to go to treatment, and she was clear when she said, "I'm talking inpatient or intensive outpatient." She knew I still needed to work. I again was talking for my life, telling her I could do it - that I would gain weight. She looked at me and said, "I'll give you one last shot. Show me you can gain weight." I did. Hasn't been an issue since. I knew when Amanda started talking that directly and wasn't backing down, something was about to shift if it wasn't me. I just made sure I was the one who shifted! I am SO grateful for her tough love. We have talked about those times since. We laugh at my antics and celebrate the growth and progress.

As Amanda and I worked together, we were able to just be straight with each other. It has been a working relationship with a counselor like none I have ever had. We have had some HARD conversations. She has taken me places I had never gone before, discovered things I never knew were there, and helped me fight for healing and not quit until it came. At the time of this writing Amanda and I have been working together for over 11 consecutive years. That's a LOT of work! She moved out of state in 2015, and thanks to the advances of technology and practice, we have been able to continue our work via the internet. When she told me she was leaving, I was sad, as was she. She said she knew I would need a little more time to adjust and process, so she told me earlier than others.

I had the option to discontinue altogether (NOT an option though tempting), start over with someone else at the agency (eh - maybe), or "follow her" to SC and continue online, not knowing how long all the logistics would take. I thought about the options, but decided I wasn't starting over with anyone else, and quitting wasn't an option, so we had about a three-week break while she got things set up. We were able to continue much sooner than originally expected. And because of that strong foundation we really haven't missed a beat.

We are now to the point where therapy has "shifted" as we look to wind down and eventually terminate. That thought alone has been scary and exciting and full of the unknown while stirring many emotions. I have told her, however, that when that termination day comes, it will be done in person. I will drive to South Carolina to see her. There is NO way, after all this time, it's going to be done just by signing off the internet. I literally owe my life and well-being to her, her patience, her skill, her professionalism, her tenacity, her belief in me, and her courage to take me where I needed to go when I didn't want to go there. There are no words to express the role she has played in my life in watching me go from being in a cocoon to a monarch butterfly being free.

This much I know...in our darkest times we need at least one person to come alongside us, walk with us, challenge us, and show us what is possible. And sometimes that person is a counselor, and it's okay to not be okay.

Chapter 10

Love Found Me!

It was late 2013. I was scrolling Facebook during lunch and saw something that piqued my interest: - an ad for a movie about the late Christian musician Rich Mullins. The movie folks were looking for volunteers to help find venues to show the movie. In November 2013, Mom and I had gone to a church in the area to see the Christian rock group Petra. I contacted the concert host venue and asked about hosting the movie coming out. It was called "Ragamuffin." It didn't take long for a date to be secured. As it turned out, some of the leadership at the church had gone to the same college as Rich Mullins and one knew Rich. Little did I know that watching the movie would have such a profound impact on my life. This movie would be another significant moment.

The first 20 minutes of the movie were difficult to watch. There was a LOT in the story that just struck home, and I wasn't ready to let on to others. I did a lot of secret wiping of tears during the movie. While I didn't want to let others know, my heart was slowly dying, and God was doing CPR. I just didn't know it yet.

I enjoyed sharing the movie with my siblings when they came to visit, and I ended up seeing the movie four times in the course of the next 6-8 months. Each time, I got something new out of it. Each message was massaging my heart, but I didn't know where it was leading, and each message built on the one prior. Soon, it all began to make sense.

In late summer, there started to be Facebook questions around the movie and "continuing the conversation" of the themes of the movie. The movie producer, along with the family and friends of

Rich Mullins, announced they were going to do a "Ragamuffin Retreat" to continue the discussion about the movie themes of masks, authenticity, living a life of reckless abandon, and the love of God. I was SO ready for that. Throughout the year, I felt as if I was starting to sink into a hole. The things my counselor and I were dealing with were painful, and I didn't know how to handle it. I was hurting, feeling unlovable and unwanted. And my eating disorder was in full swing.

The retreat was mid-October, and while internally I desperately wanted to go, it took a bit for me to finally commit to attending it. I was torn with doing something else but knew I was meant to be at the retreat. When I finally relented and registered, my anxiety rose. However, so did my silent hope that something would bring relief from the inner hell that was my mind.

One of the coolest parts of each retreat is the private Facebook room that opens about two weeks before retreat. It's an opportunity to begin building community by finding out who's attending, making new friends, sharing our stories, prayer requests, questions, making plans, and just getting to know one another. By the time the actual retreat rolls around we know names and faces and a little about each other. It avoids the awkward introductions upon arrival. I truly believe this one feature builds the foundation long before the first car pulls into the campground. Registration is more like a family reunion rather than a first introduction.

I lurked in the retreat "room" for two days before I said much past responding to other's comments and posts. People were sharing their stories, and I felt my heart pounding outside of my chest. but I still didn't share. I was hesitant, as I was just coming to grips with my story as it was, identifying what Bobby did to me as rape. It took a while for me to be able to say, "Bobby raped me." That was one of the things my counselor and I were dealing with that year - owning my story. So, to watch everyone share their stories made me want to have the same courage, but the mental demons were screeching loudly. and it took a while to fight through them.

I still remember the morning I finally broke through. It was 4:30a, and I took my computer to the dining room on the other end of the house. With coffee in hand and more in the pot, I started to type. It took 30 minutes or more to type my introduction and post it. My leg was bouncing, I'm confident my blood pressure was up, and my breathing was shallow. I was about to blow the cover on everything that had been my life, and I just "knew" someone would respond in a negative way. I was so positive of that "fact" that when I finally took a deep breath, gulped loud enough for the entire house to hear, and hit "post", I spent the rest of the day checking Facebook every hour (or more often), holding my breath to see what people said. I was waiting for it. I was expecting it. It wouldn't have been anything new. Rejection. Ridicule. Blame.

And I kept waiting.

And waiting.

All day. Numerous replies were made. I still waited. Until I realized, it just wasn't going to happen. Not one single comment was negative or degrading or blaming. Instead, they were encouraging, applauding what they called "courage" to share my story, sharing my pain and heartache and wanting to just give me a hug. It was at that moment when hope started to break through the wall I had once again built around my heart.

The day of retreat finally came. To say my trepidation was high is an understatement. I was desperate. I knew on the inside, but I was trying to hide it on the outside. Once I had made the commitment to go on the retreat, I had told my counselor to "get me ready." I still remember the day I looked at her with a forlorn look in my eyes and said, "I just want to be authentic." She and I spent six weeks - six counseling sessions - working through my anxiety, fears, desires and hesitations. By the time the retreat came around, I "thought" I was ready. Or at least ready enough to go and hope God did something. My retreat experience was later described by one of the team members as a "Hail Mary" of sorts, hoping to find that God and His kids could really love me.

I was in my own world that first retreat. I look back now and wish I had been more attentive to others there and gotten to know them better. However, I also quickly realize I had to stay focused on what I was there to do, because I would not be where I am today had I not stayed laser focused on the task at hand: healing.

Each session built on the next. At retreat, we broke up into triads for small group discussion. I had been very open with my story and everyone knew what was going on in my heart. In a lot of ways, when I had an emotional reaction, I felt like the entire group knew what was going on. Then, on Saturday afternoon, something just broke in me. Or broke through is a better way to put it

You have to be careful what you pray for. I had gone into retreat extremely broken, and in many ways desperate, barely holding on by a thread. I had been starting to admit to my story the entire year, and it was a very hard pill to swallow. The enemy had convinced me that I had gone too far for God, that what is written in the Bible is "good enough for everyone else but not for me." I had convinced myself that I was the "holy exception."

My yearning, desire, and desperation for a breakthrough can be seen in what I wrote in my journal Saturday morning. It sets the scene for what happened later.

"Lord, I don't know what today brings, but bring it. Slay me. Break me. Transform me. Begin the new work in me. May today be the turning point. I'm broken enough that I don't care anymore. I don't care if I cry. I don't care if others see me cry. I don't care if I finally just fall apart. I want to. I need to. You want me to. Capture me today. Now."

Like I said...be careful what you pray for!

Throughout the rest of the day, it seemed God was just setting me up. Things said by the speakers hit a nerve. The topics of the sessions hit a nerve (forgiveness, community, reckless faith, scars). "Everywhere I go I see You" took on a new meaning. And then, in the middle of the afternoon, it happened.

Up to this point, I had held my tears inside. I feared I would lose control when I was crying. Having an eating disorder and being a control freak, losing control of my emotions was NOT on my top list of things to do (although I knew I needed it). One of the team members did a guided imagery as she led her session on forgiveness. In it we talked about forgiving ourselves, forgiving the offender, and accepting forgiveness. During the imagery something happened inside me. The dam broke. I started to weep. Then I cried. Then I ugly cried, and it became more of a hard bawling and uncontrollable sobbing. My group, my triad, just encircled me, put their arms around me, and just held me. No judgments. No ridicule. No guilt. No shame. They were WITH me in my grief and just let God do His thing. Decades of tears came flooding out that night and no one was going to stop it. I was crying - heaving - sobbing - for a good 5-10 minutes. Everyone in the place heard and knew. Yet no one flinched.

Even the speaker said, "it seems God is working so let's just let Him work," and the small groups just continued to talk and pray. I call it my "sacred moment of release." I finally accepted my story. You see, up until this point, I was still struggling with denial, not calling things what they were, and CERTAINLY not emotionally connected to the gravity of the events. To finally let loose of the denial - the lies - and to even go so far as to let others in, was a HUGE step for me.

Later that afternoon, I wrote in my journal a dialogue after it was all said and done. It was the written record of what happened in my mind's eye when I broke down. The little girl in me was released and the adult Sue took over and gave it to God. Here is that journal entry:

(adult to child) "You've carried this weight too long. You helped me survive, and I thank you. You were strong. You were brave. You protected. You fought. And now it's time for you to rest. You can breathe now. You can be a little girl. You can relax, and play, and run, and laugh...and just BE."

(child to adult) "I'm tired. I don't just need a break. I need it to be over. I quit. I can't do this anymore. I need you to take this. You're the adult. You're an adult now. It's your turn. It's your responsibility. It's yours."

(adult to child) "Go. Go be a little girl. I release you. Go run and laugh and jump and shout and play...and just be. For the first time in your life...just...BE! No pressure, no expectations, no rules, no guilt, no shame. Be innocent. Just...BE. Whatever that means, whatever that looks like. Whatever you need to do for you...just do it. It's my turn to protect you now. Let me do for you what you did for me. Let me take care of you now."

(Jesus to adult) "Come to me. You...who are weary and heavy laden. Come to me in your sorrow and your anguish and your confusion and pain and bewilderment...and everything else. Just come. I've been waiting. I've been here the whole time. Now...run to me. Let me wrap my arms around you and hold you tight. I know you feel naked and hollow and empty and lost without the baggage - without the weight - without all the wrong expectations. And that's okay. I will fill you up. Just come.

"I was waiting outside the woods. I saw it all. And I will use it - not just can, I WILL - for I AM! I AM in your past. I AM with you in your present, and I AM already in your future. I AM working, healing, loving, redeeming. I AM with you. I AM loving you. I AM leading you. I AM guiding you. I AM using you.

"So just sit with me. It's okay to be silent. It's okay to cry. It's okay to weep. It's just okay. Because you are okay. Because...I. AM. HERE. - Jesus"

The next day was the last day of retreat. I felt lighter, happier. There was a tired buoyancy to me. I was emotionally exhausted yet felt freer. I was more open to others. I was hugging others more. I was letting myself feel more than before. Something had shifted. I had found some hope.

By the time Sunday morning was over, I went up to the movie director, who had ended the retreat with these words: "Jesus Christ loves you and is absolutely crazy about you." I looked him in the eye and through a tear-stained face said, "This is the first time I actually believe it!" Philippians 1:6 is used at retreat each year, and it was said again at the end of the first retreat: "I am confident of this, that He who began a good work in you will complete it until the day of Christ Jesus." I drove home in quiet reflection, not quite sure what had just happened but knowing something deep had begun. That "good work" was just starting!

My last journal entry from retreat says it best. Just like a child interacts with his/her father, I found myself interacting with God the same way.

> "Beyond description.
>
> "Last day. A milestone in my life. Don't expect words for a while, for right now it defies description. Don't expect anything...just let me be in the moment...for as long as I want...for as long as I need...for my Daddy is holding me tight and I don't want to let go.
>
> "Daddy. Hold me Daddy. Lift me higher Daddy. Hug me Daddy. Tighter Daddy - I can't feel you. Walk with me Daddy. Take my hand Daddy. Daddy, I have a question.

"God is no longer far off. He's here. He sees. He knows. He longs. He waits...not from a distance but right next to me instead.

"So, what has happened here? I let go. I let go of ALL the anger and hurt and disappointment I have been holding onto for years. I broke down. I didn't have to have it all together. I didn't have to be fixed - or fix - anything or anyone. I could just BE! And God found me. Because He was there all the time.

"I will weep, for it's a mourning process and there is much to mourn - a lost childhood, lost time - but I was lost AND NOW I'M FOUND! So, weep, and cry, and wail, and write, and sit, and BE. BE in the moment. BE with Me. And let ME be with you. Give yourself the grace to just do what you need to do for you."

I hoped something special had started that weekend. So many things that were addressed at Retreat spoke loudly to me. I was eager to see Amanda the week after I got back. She had invested so much time into helping me get ready for retreat that I wanted to share my experience with her. There was SO much packed into the messages at retreat that it took a while to even be able to begin verbalizing a little of what happened. I had been journaling all weekend and was certainly caught up in my own little world. I don't say that as a negative thing. Instead, as one of the staffers said, "You came to work, and you were focused on that." They call retreat "open heart surgery without the anesthesia," and it was true to form.

Amanda and I had a sense that something big was going to happen...that we would get a big bump from retreat, so we planned, and scheduled a two-hour session so we could take our time and unpack the weekend. I could just share at my own pace. Man were we smart to do that!

The easiest way I found was to just start reading my notes and journal entries. She just sat back and listened, wiped a few tears, asked a couple questions here or there, but mainly just marveled at all God had done in three days.

There was another pivotal point at the 2015 Walking Stick Retreat called "The Disappointing Messiah." The entire weekend looked at ways we have been disappointed by God when He doesn't act how we want Him to act. I had owned my story the previous year and was digging into it, but I had not let myself just cry over everything. I had told my counselor numerous times, "I'm afraid I'll start to cry and never stop." I did NOT want to feel the pain, but not feeling the pain was hurting me through my eating disorder. Pain has a way of finding an escape route, usually through some type of self-harming behavior like an addiction or issues with the law.

During the retreat, in a way only God can orchestrate, my "sacred moment of release" came. My fear of crying and not stopping was semi-realized. I sobbed. I cried. I wailed. I took deep gasps of air for that's how hard I was crying…for 10-15 minutes…with 30 other people around who knew what was going on…and no one said a negative word about it. In fact, one person came over while I was crying, quietly put his arm around me, and I later found out he had quietly prayed "Whatever it is, God, put it on me."

We were to write on a rock the names of the chains which had been binding us, keeping us from being free. I wrote "Emotions. Pain. Hurt. Seclusion. Fear. Comfort." Then we were to go outside and hurl that rock over the side of a hill, burying it there and leaving it there. When I went outside my only thought was "hurl this baby." I probably threw it a good 20 yards, and it felt SO great! For me, that sealed the deal.

Again, upon my return from Retreat, Amanda and I had a two-hour session. And again, we marveled at all God had done and the softness which was evident on my face. We knew God was continuing to do His "good work" in me, and we wanted to be sure to follow.

Amanda had said at one point that we easily see a six-month bounce from Retreat. Over time that bounce has lessened because I am experiencing more healing.

During the next four years, there were things God did in my life through Retreat; things, which I now see, have become building blocks for traveling the space between. I discuss those lessons in the second half of the book as they have been the bridge of the space between.

This much I know…God does His deepest work in our hearts when we are most desperate.

The Space Between

Introduction

The space between. What IS the space between? What on earth are we talking about?

We're all constantly in-between destinations. What encompasses your day is the space between waking up and going to bed. The trip to the store is the space between making a shopping list and packing away the groceries. Your time at college (if you decided to go), is the space between choosing a career and starting a career. You get the idea.

When we're talking about our stories, the space between is that gap, that time of questioning and anger and confusion and doubt and…and... and....whatever else you can think of. It's the gray area of uncertainty, of wondering what the point is. The space between is the search for the answer to the most basic question of life: why?

Why did things happen to you? Why didn't someone stop it? Why didn't GOD stop it? Why did God allow the hurt? Why is it taking so long to heal? Why can't I just forget and move on? Why, why, WHY?!

I've asked all those questions...and hundreds more. In my journey toward healing and recovery, there is MUCH that makes no sense to me. I've spent a L O N G time in the space between, but I've learned a few things in the process.

Process. That's a word I used to HATE! I wanted to be DONE! I didn't want to have to take the journey; I just wanted to reach the destination! I didn't know I had to give myself grace to deal with things little by little, before the healing could take root. I have since learned that to rush the "process" is to short-change yourself. To build on sand and not a sure foundation. Something worth having is worth waiting for...working for...fighting for. Healing is no different.

Over the next few chapters, I want to share what I learned on my journey... the things that filled the space between hurting and healing. I hope it helps you along the way.

Chapter 11

Own Your Story

I sat online with Amanda. It was March 2016. My "sacred moment of release" had just been a few months prior, and I was unknowingly embarking on the hardest year for me emotionally. My eating was going off again, and this time Amanda was relentless about recommending a dietician. I tried to stall and sidestep for a few weeks, but she was not letting it go. I remember finally looking at her and saying, "Is it really that bad?"

Isn't that the question we all ask? Folks in our lives may be telling us things - painful things, things we don't want to hear - and that voice in our head whispers "It's not THAT bad. They're exaggerating."

We wish. We try to convince ourselves. We get defensive. We get argumentative. But deep down, we know they're right. Yet we deny.

Have you ever stopped to wonder why we deny what we inwardly know to be true? Just thinking about THAT is painful because we come face-to-face with sin. Denial is sin because it's living a lie. I know that sounds harsh, and I didn't look at it that way when I was in the middle of it, so let me explain.

The enemy comes to steal, kill, and destroy, according to John 10:10. When we walk in the truth, we shine the light of Christ, and obviously that is at odds with the mission of the enemy. So, the enemy wants to keep us in the dark, in denial, and in sin, separated from God's best for us. When we face our "stuff" we live out 1 John 1:9: "If we confess our sins, he is faithful and just and will forgive us our sins and purify us from all unrighteousness."

When I was trapped in my eating disorder, long before I called it that, I lied. I lived a life of deception, as is the case with most addictions. People would ask if I ate, and I would respond yes, saying I had eaten. That wasn't the lie. When pushed for what I ate, I made up something so it seemed I had eaten more than a bag of chips I may have had. And later, someone would ask something similar, and I soon found myself thinking "I'm tired of keeping track of what I told whom." I certainly wasn't walking in the light. Instead, I was lurking in the shadows.

Denial becomes a double whammy. We're first in sin because of the denial, but the original issue remains. So, now we not only have to deal with the denial, but we must also deal with the issue over which we were IN denial! It quickly becomes a sticky spider web, from which it is difficult to escape. I wish I could give you a magic formula to break through denial, but there isn't such a thing as far as I know.

Why do we stay in denial? Why do we not want to face the truth? What do we fear so much...or cherish too much...to break free? I think the main answer is the same: insecurity. We fear being hurt more, being exposed, being embarrassed, being labeled, being dismissed. We fear we won't be accepted or loved. Those fears make us feel insecure. And when we feel insecure, we stay in things which are familiar to us, because it's safe and predictable. We cherish insecurity because it's secure to us.

It's been said we don't change until the pain to change is less than the pain to stay the same. So, what is that pain? What does it take to change? The answer is different for each person, yet there are some commonalities.

The pain is wrapped in all kinds of emotions: fear, embarrassment, shame, doubt, anger. Our self-talk isn't exactly positive and encouraging. It instead tends to ridicule, blame, demean, and undercut ourselves. The cycle perpetuates itself and we go down the slippery slope of convincing ourselves we are worthless, have nothing to offer, and have no one who truly cares about us. With all this garbage swirling in the cesspool, we begin to live the "self-fulfilling prophecy," and live in our familiar hell, not knowing there is another world out there within our grasp. It's no wonder we live in denial when we've totally lost touch with ourselves and the truth of who we truly are.

A close companion to denial is minimizing. You might know it by other terms: "blowing it off," "no big deal," "don't worry about it," and "that's okay." When we minimize something - consider it less than it really is - we're downplaying the situation and its effects. Doing so causes harm to ourselves and others. It hurts us because when we minimize, we deny the degree of hurt we experienced from a situation, and that equates to self-talk which says, "I don't matter as much as you do, so I'll let you off the hook." The other person is also hurt when we minimize how they wronged us because they are being told their behavior is acceptable and not harmful. Therefore, they are not held accountable for their behavior. Minimizing is sometimes more harmful than denial because minimizing is a conscious decision to deny our own worth.

How do we move from what we know - denial and minimizing - to acknowledgment of what we're trying to avoid? There's no easy answer. It's not as easy as do this, that, and the other thing. While there are no clear-cut steps to take to move from denial to acknowledgement, there are some things you will find yourself experiencing which gently move you in the direction you want to move.

ACCEPTANCE

Who doesn't want to feel accepted? Is that not part of the human condition - to have a place where you feel you "belong?" But what does it mean to be accepted? When we say we don't feel accepted, or "they don't accept me the way I am", what we're really saying is "I can't be me around those people." What do we feel or experience to lead us to that conclusion? How do we know?

First, "trust your gut." We've all heard that phrase. Each person has a keen sense of connection and can identify when something feels right and when it doesn't. Unfortunately, in the present-day situation of bullying, everyone is sizing up the other person or group for a while, wondering whom can be trusted. It's a process which can't be rushed and must be honored, for it leads to relationships which tend to last for quite a while, for not only are YOU looking for acceptance, but so is the other person with whom you connect. It's a two-way street.

What kind of conversations do you have with someone? What do they talk about or ask about? For me, if I hear "you should" come out of their mouth, my guard goes up. Are they telling me what to do? Is it a "you should give them a call" in an encouraging way or is it a "you should know better" condemnation? One supports and challenges, one tears down and destroys. Language and words tell the story in the acceptance arena.

Do the words, looks, and tone of voice they use reflect encouragement, excitement, and interest, or judgment, sarcasm, and ridicule? In short, do they build you up or tear you down?

Maybe they're "neutral" and don't really indicate either way. They just go with the flow and aren't caught up by anything or anyone. That's not necessarily bad either. Having a drama- free life goes a long way in having stable ground upon which to build.

The bottom line is, there is no standard of measure in feeling someone is accepting of you. Now let me quickly say here that "accepting" and "agreeing with" are two VERY different things. Acceptance should NEVER be based on a person agreeing with you. Life would get boring in a HUGE hurry! But, if someone makes you feel encouraged and positive and challenged in things, without also leaving you feeling judged, ridiculed, or torn down in any way, it seems safe to say they are accepting of you. They may not agree with every point of view you have, but they also don't make that a condition of relationship.

It seems these days with "tolerance" and "inclusion" as buzz words, we have tried to equate those values to agreeing with someone. Acceptance is based on love. Agreeing with someone is based on opinion. I'd MUCH rather have a relationship built on love than whether we agree on everything. Love is stable. Agreeing with someone changes with the topic. The goal is stability in relationships, not fear based on approval.

FELLOWSHIP

When we have people in our lives who enjoy being with us, quirks and all, our level of insecurity in relationships drops. When we don't feel alone, have a support system, and can just "be" with people and not have to explain anything, we find our emotions tend to start relaxing, and as the emotions relax the guards drop. Suddenly it's a little safer to start looking at things on a deeper level. We have "our tribe." However, none of that comes without risk.

We have to risk letting down the guard. Here's where you must "trust your gut." We really DO have a good sense of people we can trust and people we can't, and we must trust ourselves that our radar isn't broken. Think about your current circle of relationships - church, clubs, school, small group, work, family, friends. My guess is there's at least one person in that mix with whom you find yourself a little more honest and open than the others. Perhaps you even ask for advice, or you are asked for yours. That's a great place to start. Dip your toes in the sand, lower your mask a bit, and watch what God does.

For me, my first taste of REAL fellowship came at the Walking Stick Retreat program. I had always had trouble connecting with folks because most of them, in one way or another, demonstrated I wasn't "good enough," and it was going to be their job to "fix" me. Well, I didn't need fixing; I needed God's healing. I didn't want to be someone's "project." I wanted to be someone's friend and let them be mine. It wasn't until I got involved in the retreats that I began to realize I could be "me" - whoever that was at any given moment - and everyone was okay with that. No one left, no one got scared away, and no one said they had the answer. They just wanted to love on me and figure it out together, trusting that God had the answer and the timing. They were content to just come along for the ride and watch God work. THAT is the essence of fellowship: walking the same road, often without saying a word, knowing just presence is the best support possible, because it's about the other person, not you. When you find safe fellowship, you will feel a sense of belonging, and when you find a safe place to belong, it becomes natural to start letting more of the "real" you show.

LOVE

Fellowship leads to love. When we've found acceptance, let down our guards, and entered into vulnerable relationship with another, the next realistic outcome is love. True love. Pure love. Dare I say it...unconditional love.

We've twisted love. Love has many meanings, and there are many types of love. We "love" ice cream and we "love" a friend. We also "love" a vacation and we "love" our family. With each use of the word we describe a relationship, a level of depth. However, when we get past the colloquialisms of a common word and get to the root, we uncover a depth of intimacy and commitment.

When we truly love someone in a non-sexual way, we value them. We treasure them. We WANT to be with them, enjoy them, share with them, learn from them, speak into their lives, and let them speak into ours. We appreciate who they are, not what they do. We look out for their well-being instead of just our own. Paul put it this way in Philippians 2:3-4: "Do nothing out of selfish ambition or vain conceit, but in humility consider others better than yourselves. Each of you should look not only to your own interests but also to the interests of others."

Now that's a tall order...do NOTHING out of selfish ambition or vain conceit. I think the "vain conceit" part is the hardest. We can well identify, at least to ourselves, when we're doing something in selfish ambition. We may not like to admit it or own it (remember, we're talking about going from denial to acceptance of our stories), but we might know it deep down. However, that vain conceit part gets to the core. We may try to pull it over on someone or pass it off as something that it's not, but if we really strip it down, what do our actions reveal? If you truly love someone, you will want to do things simply because you want to show them value, appreciation, and worth. It doesn't matter if you get anything in return. You're looking out for their interests, not yours.

I believe we all yearn for that type of love. We search for it, and when we keep coming up empty, we settle for second best. If we can't find true love and acceptance, we settle for being used by someone. Unfortunately, I settled for this in high school. I had a boyfriend on and off for most of my high school years. I found my security by having a boyfriend, so I could at least go to the dances and be seen. I am not proud of that, but I am thankful at our 25th Class reunion that I was able to talk to Garry privately, apologize, and ask forgiveness. What was wonderful about that moment is he also admitted to using me. We used each other's presence to increase our sense of self-worth. In the end, we were both insecure and in search of true love. I am thankful Garry found the love of his life and married her, raising a family. Garry has since passed away, but I am ever so thankful we had that chance to talk, to be real, to show true love and value to each other, even if it was 25 years later.

The relationships we allow in our lives reflect how we view ourselves. If we let down our guards and cultivate true relationships with give and take, acceptance, vulnerability, and trust, we value ourselves the way God values us. If we allow weak, shallow, performance-based relationships to take root, we short-change ourselves and demean and devalue ourselves as an heir of God.

GRACE

True Christ-like love cannot exist without grace. What is grace? Grace is more than a prayer before we eat. Grace is getting what we don't deserve.

By virtue of the human condition, we all deserve death. We are wretched, ruthless, selfish, sinful people. The Bible says in James 2:10, "For whoever keeps the whole law and yet stumbles at just one point is guilty of breaking all of it." In other words, in the eyes of God, if we break one of the 10 Commandments (the Law) once, we are guilty of breaking all of them. NO ONE is perfect. As the Bible says in Romans 3:10, ""There is no one righteous, not even one; there is no one who understands; there is no one who seeks God."

That sounds hopeless. I mean, if we've already screwed up in the eyes of God, what's the point? Is there any hope? YES! BECAUSE OF THE GRACE OF GOD! Because God does not give us what we deserve - death - we have purpose, life, and hope. We only have it because Jesus took the punishment from God, which we deserve. The best part is after God's standard of perfection was satisfied, God raised Jesus from the dead and when we place our trust in Him - when we let Him have control of our lives - we can then tap into the ever-abundant grace of God to help us when we need it most. And we REALLY need it when we try to love others the way Jesus wants us to love them.

Grace is not getting what we deserve, and our source of grace is our relationship with Christ. Let's break it down in the context of a relationship. Say you've done something or said something to offend a dear friend. That person is angry, hurt, and feeling betrayed. Your heart sinks because you know you blew it. You really don't think you can do anything to make it right. But when grace starts to flow, a special strength is given to allow the hard conversations to take place without judging, condemning, or ridiculing the other. Remember what we talked about when we were talking about acceptance? Here it is in action. Grace allows room for reconciliation and forgiveness. It doesn't mean the hurt didn't happen; it just means the hurt doesn't have to end the relationship.

It is important to understand, however, that grace does not mean being a doormat. Grace is not permission. Grace is bypassing what would be "justifiable" and choosing to let it go. It doesn't mean harm did not happen. It doesn't necessarily mean there aren't consequences for the behavior. It doesn't mean there's a free license to just keep doing whatever you want to do. Grace extends mercy instead of demanding retribution. It makes room for growth instead of harboring a grudge. Grace remembers the human condition and Who can help us manage it best. Grace is a gift we give each other when we love each other. Because we know we're going to need it ourselves at any moment.

We are talking about the things we experience that will help us move from denying our stories to accepting our stories. To move from denial to acceptance requires surrounding ourselves with people who will accept us and love us and extend grace to us. People are messy. Our lives are messy. We're going to hurt people, and other people are going to hurt us. There is no hope for any peace in our lives if we move from relationship to relationship expecting to get hurt, and when it happens, putting up the wall a little more. We pull back yet another step, isolating ourselves, making us an easy target for the enemy to "steal, kill, and destroy."

To break free from our past requires first that we own our stories, and to own our stories we MUST move past denial. Owning our stories is scary and painful and seemingly unbearable without a support system to help. That support system comes from friends and other important people in our lives...people with whom we have built hardship-withstanding relationships because we have taken the risk to let down our walls, be authentic, experience acceptance and love through fellowship, and accept the gift of grace. Once that gift of grace is flowing in our lives, the next part of navigating "the space between" is more bearable.

Chapter 12

Grieve Your Story

My dear friend Billy Sprague, the one with whom I had the conversation in Colorado, used to give me "recommended reading" lists. Frederick Buechner was always on his list. That turned me on to Buechner and I searched out more of his books. One of my all-time favorites is "Telling Secrets." My copy of it has more highlights than a college textbook! Little did I know when I first read it the profound - almost prophetic - influence it would have on my life almost two decades later.

In the book, Buechner writes, "Even the saddest things can become, once we have made peace with them, a source of wisdom and strength for the journey that still lies ahead." (Frederick Buechner (1991). "Telling Secrets", Harper San Francisco). There is one prepositional phrase in there which acts has the kingpin. Do you see it? "Once we have made peace with them." Remembering our grade school grammar, a preposition is a pre-position...what comes after doesn't happen until the pre-position is met. It is climbing the mountain of that prepositional phrase that catapults us in our journeys.

In our quest to make peace with our stories, we are setting ourselves up for pain. That sounds a little crazy since we've tried to avoid the pain all along. Nevertheless, like the Marines say, "there's only one way off the island," and the road to freedom runs through the pain, not around it. It takes courage to be willing to face the pain head on and let the pain be felt before letting it go. It is not for the faint of heart and the temptation to "stay with the familiar" is strong, but to do so only means freedom will never be complete.

GIVE YOURSELF PERMISSION TO FEEL

Complete freedom was a wish for me...another one of those "always just out of reach, good enough for everyone else but not for me" things in my life. I doubted I could - or would - ever be fully free. My struggle was all I had ever really known, and even after I gave name to the issues, it seemed the struggle only intensified. Such is the nature of spiritual war. Think about it for a minute. You are a child of God purchased with the blood of His son, Jesus Christ, who defeated the enemy (Satan) through dying on the cross and being resurrected three days later. Satan doesn't like that. God's desire is for everyone to be with Him in Heaven and Christ's sacrifice made the way for God's justice to be leveled, so we didn't have to pay the price for sin.

There has been a war raging since the beginning of time when Satan was thrown out of Heaven for his pride in wanting to be equal with God. Ever since then, Satan wants to hurt God by taking away from God as many humans as possible. Satan wants people to believe his lies and turn away from God. We are held captive in our lies, believing all the things that hold us back from being all God created us to be. Lies like "Nobody cares," "God couldn't love me," "I'm worthless," "I can't do that," "I deserved that," "I'll never be free like them," "I may as well give up," "It's my fault I was abused," "I'll never amount to anything." The list could go on. When we think like this, we are not walking in the power God has provided for us, and Satan is happy to have us on the side of the road watching life pass us by, not pursuing the things of God.

It is a conscious decision to face what has been avoided all this time, and when we decide to deal with things head on, Satan takes notice and the fight intensifies. We must be resolute in our determination, focus, and commitment to take off our masks, be honest, and let ourselves feel real emotions, very possibly for the first time in our lives. When I hit that point, my mantra became "a manageable level of tolerable existence is no longer an option." I had to remind myself of that frequently, and it kept me coming back to my counselor's office for more, knowing it would take me where I needed to go.

Dealing with emotions and letting go will look different for each person.

HAVE A FUNERAL AND GRIEVE

When we deal with our emotions, we're having a funeral. We are grieving all we have lost. When you go to a funeral, there are tears. It's okay to cry and sob and wail and moan. When we let our hearts thaw, we are taking God to the dead places in our lives. He wants to go there, but He won't force Himself. Once we grant Him access, however, He gives us resurrection on the other side of the mountain.

The key to having a funeral and grieving is having patience with yourself. There is no timeline for this, and it's not going to be a "one and done" event. It is a process. There's that word again. There will be ebbs and flows along the way, what feel like steps forward and then steps back. Keep going. Everyone rests while they are on a journey, and the journey of feeling emotions is a hard climb, especially when they've been frozen for so long. There are so many things to discover in the process...like it's okay to feel whatever you are feeling. The feeling itself is not wrong or bad. The challenge is learning to honor that emotion and deal with it appropriately. For a while, it may feel overwhelming and you may feel lost in it all. Have a support system in place to help you deal with it all. I highly recommend having a counselor as you embark on this. There are so many tentacles that come out once the ice is thawed. Not only are you truly feeling for the first time, but then, as you dig into the feelings, you go back to the events which brought all the pain and have to discover what feelings are tied in that event, deal with those feelings, and make peace with them. In making peace with the feelings, we make peace with our stories.

Notice I say make peace with the feelings. There will always be parts of our stories that hurt and make us cry, even decades after the event. By no means does making peace mean we are downplaying the severity of whatever happened. Bobby raped me. Period. That changed my life in too many ways. I can never change that event, and I can still be angry about it. However, I don't have to let the anger destroy my life anymore. THAT is the difference. It's okay to be angry and call the event wrong. That is speaking truth. But in dealing with all the tentacles of it, I have come to peace with the truth that the rape was not my fault, that I am worthwhile and have much to offer, and that God can use my story to help someone else. Those were all lies I had to work through - tentacles of the misdirected anger.

LET IT GO

The other hard part of this entire process of going from numb to thawed is letting go. Hear me clearly: LETTING GO DOES NOT MEAN FORGETTING. There is a HUGE difference. Up to this point, we have tried to forget the pain. If we just ignore the pain, it will go away, right? Wrong. That's how we got to where we are now. Pain has a way of finding an escape hatch, and it's usually not healthy unless we are dealing with it directly. I will never downplay what has happened to you. As mentioned in the previous chapter, if we want true healing, we can't deny it, and we can't minimize it. What happened to us, and how we feel is valid. We have every right to feel whatever it is we are feeling. Feel it. Honor it. Grieve it. And then let it go. Throw it over the side of a hill and leave it there. If we do not let go of what has hurt us, we stay chained to it. When we are in chains, we are not free. There will be more tears and emotions in letting go. There will be tears and emotions in everything as the heart thaws. Just like thawing a package from the freezer is a slow process, so is thawing emotions. Don't rush the process. When we let it go, we give it to God, who is the only one who judges rightly, and we leave it there. We take the weight off our shoulders, and we walk in the freedom that brings. It might be something you find yourself doing multiple times a day. That's why Paul called it a "living sacrifice" - it likes to keep crawling off the altar. I think of the scene in the movie "The Shack," where the dad is carrying his daughter's body down from the mountain to bury her, and with each step, he repeats, "I forgive him." "I forgive him." "I forgive him." It's the same thing…it's a conscious choice, a heart choice, and no one can make it but you. I can tell you this, though, God DOES resurrect on the other side of the mountain, but you must go through the mountain, not around it.

Chapter 13

You ARE Valuable to God!

As I have fought for freedom, my biggest enemy has been my negative thought pattern. Everything starts with the mind. There is a reason the Apostle Paul writes in 2 Corinthians 10:5 *"...we take captive every thought to make it obedient to Christ."* For anyone who has experienced any kind of trauma, anxiety is a close companion, which never seems to want to leave. I believe it is a snare of the enemy to keep us from all God has for us. Even when we start to break free, anxiety likes to convince us things are "just beyond reach" as if the prison door has swung open, yet we stay in the cell out of fear. It took quite a while for me to feel "worthy" and "worthwhile" of fighting for me. What do I mean by that? I mean I finally set myself as the priority.

A common phrase Amanda heard uttered from my lips was "it's not worth it." She tirelessly challenged me with, "What you're really saying is YOU'RE not worth it." OUCH! It hurt because it was true. I didn't buy it for a long time. I was still stuck in denial of my story and the feelings of worthlessness which had been cast on me as a result. How could I be "worth it" when I felt anything but worthy? Because feelings lie. Feeling and being are two very different things.

Feelings are valid emotions. However, when tangled in an overwhelmed brain, feelings have the potential to become seemingly toxic. An overwhelmed brain struggles to separate the actual emotion from the intensity of the emotion. As a result, the train goes off track, and we quickly find ourselves just trying to hang on until life becomes manageable again. It is in that space where we feel worthless that we have to cling to the truth that we are worthy regardless.

Being is a state of existence. It is a truth, an anchor, and a rally point. It is the pivot point from which all things happen. Not "feeling" a fact does not make it any less of a fact. What we believe about a fact influences our actions for either good or bad.

Worth is found in identity. When I was in college, I was searching for identity and acceptance at every turn. I needed something to validate my worth, give me purpose, and prove to myself that I mattered. Amidst all the things with which I was involved, my main identity became the Greek letters I proudly wore on my clothes. At first, it was being a Little Sis of Sigma Phi Epsilon (Sig Ep), and a couple years later, it became as an active sister of Beta Sigma. Looking back, I found identity with people more than in activities because I wasn't alone. Isn't that our ultimate desire - to not be alone? When we are stuck in our stories, afraid to move, and held hostage by anxiety, the common racing thought is, "I'm alone. No one understands. No one "gets" it." Thus starts the downward spiral of isolation, which is exactly where the enemy wants us. Do you see how it all comes back to what I said at the start of this chapter? It all starts in the mind.

The fact of the matter is this: Jesus Christ is ABSOLUTELY crazy about you! When I first heard that phrase at retreat, I doubted it, scorned it, and wished it was true., However, I knew nothing more than to hold onto my hurt because I was convinced it didn't apply to me. However, over the course of the weekend, as I owned my story, I saw my belief change from being the "holy exception" to truly believing it for the first time! That belief started to change my entire thought process about being worthy. When I started to actually believe - and walk in the belief - that God cares about me and hurts over the things that have happened to me, I suddenly realized I mattered. I had worth in God's eyes, and it was slowly coming into focus in mine. Only then was it okay to begin letting down my guard around God. It was okay to let my emotions out and vent with God. I was taking the first step to being authentic and real. As I started to believe that I mattered to God and saw that reinforced through the actions of those around me, I started to believe I was worthy of love and acceptance.

When we begin to believe we are worthy, we begin to respect ourselves. Who respects something that is believed to be worthless? As the "worthless" lie is torn down, and the roots of the "worth" truth begin to sprout, things start to change. How we view ourselves starts improving. Healthy boundaries begin to take shape where once there was only a line that was crossed daily. Suddenly things that "didn't matter" become priorities, giving us courage to step out of our comfort zones. As this "holy dissatisfaction" took root in my life, my mantra with Amanda became "a manageable level of tolerable existence is no longer an option." That stake in the ground became my motivation for continuing in therapy when my anxiety and fear screamed at me to quit.

Whatever form it takes, find that stake in the ground point for you. What is the line that you will not allow yourself - or others - to cross as you fight for the respect you deserve? What is your "rallying cry" for yourself when you question and doubt your ability to stay in the fight when the emotions are louder than before? YOU are the one who must fight for you. Others can encourage you along the way and be with you through it all, but until YOU make the hardcore choice to do something about your condition, nothing will change. No one can do it for you. Nothing will change for you until you settle for yourself the issue of being worthy. Will you believe what God says about you? Believing your true worth comes down to a crisis of belief. It's something to be settled between God and yourself. Once it's settled, drive that stake in the ground and don't look back, because you don't live in that world anymore. True freedom is worth fighting for which means YOU are worth fighting for, because YOU matter to God! Period.

Chapter 14

You are HIS!

Being authentic is a difficult journey. It is not for the faint of heart. The fight is exhausting and exhilarating, wrought with peril and promise, challenged by fear, and sustained by faith. An underlying strength must be present to survive what it takes emotionally to be maskless and be real.

When I was young, I read the book <u>The Velveteen Rabbit</u> by Margery Williams. Something about that story struck a chord and stuck to my heart, only to find its way-out decades later. This excerpt says it best:

> "Real isn't how you are made," said the Skin Horse. "It's a thing that happens to you. When a child loves you for a long, long time, not just to play with, but REALLY loves you, then you become Real."
> "Does it hurt?" asked the Rabbit.
> "Sometimes," said the Skin Horse, for he was always truthful. "When you are Real you don't mind being hurt."
> "Does it happen all at once, like being wound up," he asked, "or bit by bit?"
> "It doesn't happen all at once," said the Skin Horse. "You become. It takes a long time. That's why it doesn't happen often to people who break easily, or have sharp edges, or who have to be carefully kept. Generally, by the time you are Real, most of your hair has been loved off, and your eyes drop out and you get loose in the joints and very shabby. But these things don't matter at all, because once you are Real you can't be ugly, except to people who don't understand."

The fight, struggle, doubt, confusion, pain, feelings, and questions, which started in the space between, bring us the same thing as we find the goal of our journey: hope. There is no way any sane person would have the courage to face the things buried in the heart if there wasn't some kind of "nagging optimism" as I call it. Why would anyone deal with feeling exposed and vulnerable, if there wasn't a deep desire inside to find something better - to HOPE there was more to life than the living hell that has been reality up to now? It is against the norm. Many, unfortunately, do not have the internal fortitude to face the giants, so to speak. The phrase "I have an image to uphold" is prevalent today, even if the words are not boldly spoken. Actions speak louder than words.

To have hope is to believe there is something more, something better than the present. Hope propels us, motivates us, convicts us, challenges us, and comforts us. Ultimately, it is the hope of the gospel that brings things to fulfillment. It is one thing to strive for freedom, and there is a different challenge when the struggle seems to have been won. Since God has healed my emotions, I have had to deal with "who am I without my struggle?" I have had to question a lot of the identity and questions of self-worth we looked at in the last chapter. Just as a prisoner may be a repeat offender, simply to be able to go back to the "comfortable and predictable" environment of prison because it's "all they've ever known," when we get through the muck and mire of trauma and find our way to the other side - everything we had envisioned and hoped for - now becomes reality. It can be a weird feeling. A completely new journey of self-discovery begins. The space between has a new landscape which can be equally frightening and challenging.

Everything up to this point has been with eyes looking back to then look ahead and pursue freedom. Once freedom is realized, it is still a process of looking back to then look ahead. The difference, however, is learning to live in newfound life. The same questions, doubts, and fears will try to raise their ugly heads (calling you to look back) and the conscious choice will then need to be made each day to believe what we had to choose to believe in the middle of the fight: we are worth it. We are worth being free, walking in freedom, living with healthy boundaries, identifying, honoring, and letting go of emotions, and walking in the freedom of authenticity. There will be some who don't "get it," and wonder why you are so open about whatever. Secretly, they may be wishing they had that courage, the same way you secretly wished for courage when you saw authenticity in others and yearned for it yourself, except you didn't know how to go about getting it.

FINAL THOUGHTS

Now that you have walked my journey with me, it's your turn. I'm not naive to say simply reading this book will be the magic wand to see you arrive at your destination of freedom. I've said it already, but it bears repeating: there is no magic formula for any of this and each person's journey is different. I am simply here to share my story, and hopefully, to encourage you in yours.

After the hard emotional work has brought forth its fruit of freedom, there is a greater responsibility at hand. Being free from the shackles of fear, anxiety, depression, acceptance, and negativity doesn't mean those things aren't still active. They are still there. That will not change. It's part of the human condition. Anyone who says they do not struggle with any of those things is caught up in living a masked, disingenuous life, trying to portray something that isn't there. Sound familiar?

The two most powerful words in the Bible, in my opinion, are found in the Bible 45 times: "But God." That word "but" is SO powerful. It connotes intervention, a change of direction, a redistribution of energy. They refute what we tell ourselves and are keywords needed in our arsenal of taking thoughts captive. BUT GOD breaks chains the world tells us we can't overcome. BUT GOD redeems life from death of vision and purpose due to trauma. BUT GOD gives hope during unbearable pain and heartache. BUT GOD brings freedom which cannot be broken!

God sees you, loves you, is absolutely crazy about you, believes in you, forgives you, has plans for you, and does not quit on you. It is a process, one which will not be completed until the day of Christ Jesus (Phil. 1:6), one He deemed worthy (and YOU worthy) of costing Jesus Christ His very life so that YOU can walk in the power and freedom of BUT GOD. God has made it possible for you to no longer be bound, but to be free. It is a choice you must make to walk in the truth by letting Him give you the strength and power to fight to escape from the wounds of your past, let Him heal them, and watch the wounds become scars. Scars give hope that there is healing. Your scars may be a story which will help someone else who is where you once were. My pastor once said, "What does it take to help the person behind you? You only have to be one step ahead." When we live in the BUT GOD truth of freedom, we can be that step ahead to help someone who is fighting the same fight, just as you have had people help you.

Freedom must be protected. It has been hard-fought and has cost God everything. It is not to be taken lightly or taken for granted. All the spiritual disciplines of Bible reading, prayer, fellowship, service, and giving protect that freedom. Pride will try to creep in. When the negative things to which the enemy has held us captive are uprooted and destroyed, we must take great care to be sure that "empty space" is replaced with the opposite of what once occupied it. Just because we have found freedom does not mean the enemy won't try to make us captive again. The spiritual warfare we discussed earlier is still alive and well. In many ways, we are learning for the first time with a clean slate what God truly thinks of us.

Up until now, it has been tainted with the world's stains, and we twisted it when we wore those lenses. Now that those blinders have been removed, we are on a new adventure, discovering what freedom in Christ truly means and brings. It does not mean we don't experience heartache or pain or even trauma, but it does mean we respond differently from a healthy stance, deal with things appropriately, and in grace then move on. THAT is the power of BUT GOD. That is what it means to be no longer be bound but to be free. That is what is found in the space between.

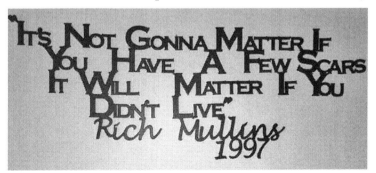

References

Bianco, Margery W and William Nicholson. The Velveteen Rabbit: Or, How Toys Become Real. New York: Avon Books, 1975. Print.

Bowles, Sue. Personal Journal Entry. 2015.

Buechner, Frederick. Telling Secrets. Harper San Francisco, 1991. Print.

Mullins, Rich. "Winds of Heaven, Stuff of Earth." Reunion, 1988. CD.

About the Author

Sue Bowles writes, blogs and speaks on eating disorder recovery and other mental health issues. Being in recovery herself, she has a passion for educating and encouraging others. She also runs mystepahead.com, a website dedicated to breaking the stigma of mental health issues.

Sue earned a Bachelor of Science degree in Speech from The Defiance College and a Master of Science from Minnesota State University: Mankato in Counseling: College Student Development. She has since worked in higher education, faith-based non-profit groups, as well as the business world. Sue is available to speak to your group regardless of size, including meetings, campus events, church groups, retreats, conferences, and seminars.

Made in the USA
Lexington, KY
29 September 2019